SHIPROCKED

First published in 2009 by
Liberties Press
Guinness Enterprise Centre | Taylor's Lane | Dublin 8 | Ireland
www.LibertiesPress.com
General and sales enquiries: +353 (1) 415 1224 | peter@libertiespress.com
Editorial: +353 (1) 415 1287 | sean@libertiespress.com

Trade enquiries to CMD Distribution
55A Spruce Avenue | Stillorgan Industrial Park | Blackrock | County Dublin
Tel: +353 (1) 294 2560 | Fax: +353 (1) 294 2564

Distributed in the United States by
Dufour Editions
PO Box 7 | Chester Springs | Pennsylvania | 19425

and in Australia by
James Bennett Pty Limited | InBooks
3 Narabang Way | Belrose NSW 2085

Liberties Press is a member of Clé,
the Irish Book Publishers' Association.

ISBN: 978–1–905483–62–4

2 4 6 8 10 9 7 5 3 1

A CIP record for this title is available from the British Library.

Set in Garamond
Printed in Ireland by Colour Books | 105 Baldoyle Industrial Estate | Dublin 13

Cover images: (top) The *Ross Revenge* (photo: courtesy of the author);
(left) Christmas Day 1987 on Caroline, with (from left to right) Chris Kennedy, John
Bibby, Steve Conway and Mike 'Coconut' Dixon (photo: John Burch Collection);
(right) 'Brothers In Arms': Chris Kennedy and Steve Conway in 1987
(photo: John Burch Collection)

SHIPROCKED

STEVE CONWAY

LIBERTIES

Contents

Author's Note

All of the events described in this book are from my own memory of how and when things happened and I have sought to present them as they seemed to me at the time, without the benefit of hindsight. In most cases, the names used are those which people broadcast under on Radio Caroline, but in a small number of cases, where particular events might cause embarrassment, I have changed the name or blurred the timeline slightly.

During the years that I was on-board Radio Caroline, there were several hundred visits by supply vessels bringing or removing staff members to or from the ship. It is not possible to mention every arrival or departure, so the reader will notice people appearing or disappearing in the narrative, and sometimes vanishing from the story, not to be mentioned again. This well represents how life was on board – someone you worked and lived closely with for months would vanish overnight, with no goodbyes, and it would only be months later that it would become obvious that they were not returning.

Likewise, during the years I was involved with the station, I worked with more than a hundred fellow broadcasters or crew members, many of whom are not mentioned here, simply because they did not happen to be involved in the events I have put into the book. All played a vital role in keeping Radio Caroline alive and at sea during a fascinating period at the end of the 1980s, and no slight is intended by their omission.

Finally, I would like to acknowledge the help of John and Anita Burch, both during the whirlwind of events described in this book and in the production of the book itself; my agent, Sarah at Seven Towers, whose editing and encouragement has been vital; my partner, Brenda, who has put up with my absence for long hours while writing and editing; Simon Maher and Ger Roe of my current employers, Phantom 105.2FM, who have both tolerated and encouraged this project; and Peter Moore and all the members of the Radio Caroline Society, who ensure that, although no longer at sea, both the ship and the radio station have survived into the modern age of satellite broadcasting.

Steve Conway
Dublin, February 2009

PROLOGUE

I was happy. The evening couldn't get much better, nor my surroundings any more ideal than they were where I was now, ensconced in a warm and softly lit studio, pleasantly full after a fine evening meal, and enjoying the music I was playing for Radio Caroline's considerable night-time audience.

It was about 10:30 PM. I had the studio lights down low and was feeling very content to be weaving my web of music in one of the nicest corners of the ship as the winds outside blew in gusts from the north-west and the sea started to get up.

I had just played Richie Valens' 'Donna', which had given me some pleasant thoughts of a girl of the same name who was awaiting my next shore leave, and, as I followed it with Robert Palmer's 'She Makes My Day', I was sure that the mood would last until bedtime.

Very abruptly, it was all gone. The lights flickered and faded. The record slowed and then stopped. And the howling of the wind and the noise of the waves had suddenly become audible above the last gasp of the dying generator. I urgently ran up the steep stairs to wake our engineer Peter Chicago, then down two flights to the storeroom where the paraffin lamps were kept.

It was a pitch-black October night, with no moon, and we were sitting close to the edge of one of the busiest shipping lanes in the world. Unlatching the big metal door leading to the outside, I headed with my lamp for the back deck to try to make sure that we would not be completely invisible to other ships in the area.

The panicked voice of a fellow crew member assailed me: 'We're going to die! That ship can't see us with our lights off! It's going to hit us, and we're all going to die!' A cluster of lights about a mile away was obviously a ship, and, judging by the angle of their red and green navigation lights, it was coming straight for us. They should be able to see us on the radar if they were monitoring it, but then again, they wouldn't be expecting an unlit ship to be directly ahead of them. I tried not to think about what would happen if they collided with us broadside on.

Hoping they had noticed us before our lights went off, I hauled myself up the last few rungs of the metal ladder on to the back deck, and held the lamp as high as I could. Chris Kennedy was on his way forward with another lamp, while Chicago was on his way down to the generator room in the bowels of the ship to see what the problem was, and if one of the spare generators could be drummed into action.

The cause of the problem was probably dirty fuel – in which case all the generators would be affected and we would be powerless for hours while the system was flushed and drained. As I waved the lamp above my head, hoping it would be seen by the other ship, I couldn't help but think about how efficient and well run the ship had been when I'd joined her less than two years earlier.

It had all been different back then, so very, very different . . .

1

FOREIGNER

MAY 1984–FEBRUARY 1987

I was nineteen when I moved to England from Dublin, crossing the Irish Sea on the Liverpool ferry, like so many millions of emigrants before me. Compared to many of those emigrants, I was very lucky: I had a year's experience in the then very new personal-computer industry, and I was on my way to a job in a small computer dealership, AP Systems in Surbiton, south London.

I was fairly successful at integrating into the British way of life, and progressed from a damp, shabby bedsit to a friendly shared flat. I got a company car, and enjoyed working for APS. I gradually made friends, and got to know London and Surrey, as well as the various customers of APS, who, as early adopters of personal computers in their businesses, needed me on call pretty much all the time.

I had a couple of almost-girlfriends, and a couple of short relationships, but my adventures with the opposite sex never quite seemed to get off the ground. I blamed this on my single-sex schooling – having been taught by the Marist Fathers at the Catholic University School in Dublin had left me ill-prepared for dealing with women – though my fairly serious nature and a fair dose of shyness also did me few favours. During my early months in London, there were many opportunities I could have taken but shied away from, not to mention the invitations that I simply didn't notice – such as the girlfriend who eventually dumped me because she kept inviting me in for 'coffee' at the end of the evening, and I kept refusing. I had taken these invitations to be simply the offer of hospitality and a warm drink when I dropped her home – and sure wouldn't it be awfully rude of me to accept and have her making coffee for me at one in the morning? I was baffled when she dumped me, saying that I obviously didn't want to be intimate.

It was the spring of 1984, pop music was going through a revival after the subdued 1970s, and the airwaves were alive with the sounds of Springsteen, Duran Duran, Cyndi Lauper, OMD, Spandau Ballet, Wham! and Frankie Goes To Hollywood. Within days of arriving in the UK, I had discovered a station where the music was good, mixing the hits of the day with an eclectic collection of rock, reggae and album tracks, where the DJs were friendly without being intrusive, and where there were few interruptions for commercials. It was Radio Caroline.

Radio in the UK was still highly regulated at this time, with only a handful of stations, and very strict rules on the amount of music that could be played each day. So there was an opportunity for Radio Caroline, which was broadcast from a ship just outside British waters, with a transmitter powerful enough to reach London and the populous south-east. Caroline had been launched – to great acclaim and commercial success – in 1964 by the reclusive businessman Ronan O'Rahilly, grandson of the famous Irish rebel. It had been on the air with a few gaps until 1980, when the ship the *Mi Amigo* gave up the ghost and sank in a fierce storm. By the time I moved to England in 1984, they were back, broadcasting in medium wave from a bigger, better ship, the *Ross Revenge*.

During my first months in London, Caroline was joined on the high seas by the brash all-American Laser 558, which played non-stop pop, in comparison to Caroline's more mixed format. Both stations had a large following, particularly in London, during that long, hot summer. In my second year in London, I dabbled in pirate radio myself, getting involved with small part-time local pirate station, South East Sound, which broadcast rock music from a transmitter in the woods above Purley on Sunday afternoons. I helped out on what was called 'site duty' – carrying the bulky equipment into the woods and helping set it up each Sunday morning, and removing it in the evening. I also got the chance to present a couple of pre-recorded shows, which I did, sounding pretty nervous, despite the coaching I had received from the other presenters.

It was through South East Sound that I came to meet John Burch, whose day-job was operations director for a large bus company in Essex but who, in his spare time, ran the biggest Caroline supporters' club, the Caroline Movement. Caroline had several million listeners and a few thousand hard-core supporters, who joined the fan clubs, swapped tapes of the station's shows, and often went on sightseeing boat trips to visit the ship. John was also involved in the fringes of the station itself: his sightseeing trips were occasionally used to ferry goods and personnel illegally to the *Ross Revenge*. I was fascinated to hear of the covert operations of the small group of people who struggled to keep the Caroline ship supplied and crewed, despite a law which outlawed any form of work or assistance for a radio ship broadcasting from international waters. I helped John computerise his club's membership records and magazine, all the while learning more about Caroline – and becoming more and more interested in it. Eventually, John persuaded me to take a trip out to sea on one of the sightseeing boats, so that I could see the source of these broadcasts which had kept me entertained for so many hours.

One foggy Sunday in December 1985, I drove through the early hours of the morning to the small town of Strood, near Chatham, on the River Medway in Kent. John had hired a small fishing boat, whose owner was willing to transport sightseers out to the pirate radio ship, despite the threat of being arrested or fined by the authorities if he was caught. And this threat was very real at that time: the British government, tired of the two radio ships seemingly operating with impunity just outside their jurisdiction, had launched a high-profile campaign to get them off the air. A government surveillance ship had been permanently stationed close to the two ships since August, chasing and arresting supply vessels from the UK, or passing details to their country of origin if they came from elsewhere. Sightseeing-boat operators were being harassed: we were leaving from Strood because the regular boat operators in the more convenient ports of Ramsgate and Margate had all been warned off.

The campaign against the pirates by the Department of Trade & Industry was costing the government a huge amount of money, but just before my trip, after several months of surveillance, they had been successful in forcing Laser 558 off the air. The crew of American DJs on the *MV Communicator*, low on food, water and fuel, had finally given up and allowed the officials to board their ship and help them sail it in to port, where it was impounded. 'One down, one to go,' the DTI announced. Although Radio Caroline was believed to be in a much better position than Laser operationally, with larger reserves of food and fuel, John felt that it was essential to keep the sightseeing trips running by hook or by crook, for reasons of morale if nothing else.

We departed Strood at about 8.30 AM and expected to reach the Caroline ship by lunchtime, but the tide and weather conditions, together with the boat owner's desire to approach on a somewhat roundabout course, caused great delays, and it was late afternoon, and getting dark, before we approached the Knock Deep, a channel through the sandbanks of the Thames estuary where the *Ross Revenge* was permanently anchored. Well hidden by the fog, we were not immediately spotted by the government ship, the *Guardline Tracker*, though John guessed that they would spot us on the radar when we came close enough. All the way out, we had been listening to Radio Caroline, and it was strange to think that we would soon be coming alongside the ship from which all this was originating, and seeing the faces behind the voices. As we closed in on the Knock Deep, the fog thickened, and the air became very still as we slid through the water. We knew that somewhere just ahead of us was the *Ross Revenge*, and that the DTI ship must be somewhere close by, but we could see nothing.

The voice of Kate Bush was now echoing out from the little radio on our fishing boat. She was singing her recent hit 'Cloudbusting', a very atmospheric track with a slow, hypnotic rhythm that seemed to blend in with our almost silent progress through the fog. And then, suddenly, ghostly lights appeared beside us in the fog and we were alongside a huge red ship bearing the name *Ross Revenge* and with a big painted Caroline logo on the side. We could see friendly faces peering out of lighted portholes, and a giant radio tower disappearing out of view into the darkness above our heads. The song came to a crescendo as we reached its source, giving our arrival an unreal and almost magical property.

Willing hands on the pirate ship quickly tied us up alongside, and John Burch hurriedly started passing over a large number of packages to the ship, taking advantage of the fact that the DTI had not yet arrived to chase us away. To our delight, the Caroline crew invited us on board, and we were given a lightning tour of the main areas of the ship. We saw the Caroline studio, the enormous record library, the newsroom and the ship's bridge before one of the DJs rushed up to tell us that the *Guardline Tracker* was approaching and would be at the ship shortly. The government were powerless to board either the radio ship or the sightseeing boat in international waters, but they could follow the sightseeing boat back and intercept us once we were back in British waters.

We said a hurried goodbye to the DJs and scrambled back overboard and down onto our little craft just as the government ship arrived close by, its searchlights blazing down on us. As we pulled away, I was left with an all-too-brief taste of what the Radio Caroline ship was like, an immense appreciation for all that these people were going through to bring good music radio to the UK, and a sudden wish that I could have stayed behind and learned more about that little community of people living such a strange and isolated life, many miles out at sea, surrounded by nothing but water and great music.

The fog lifted as we moved away from the Knock Deep, and the *Guardline Tracker* kept on our tail. John stood up in the glare of the spotlight and, taking out a megaphone, proceeded to lecture the officials on board about the right to free speech, the amount of money being wasted by the government on the blockade of the radio ships, and Caroline's right to broadcast from international waters. Our boat owner, determined not to be intercepted, took us on a zigzag course through the estuary, including over several sandbanks that would be far too near the surface for the bigger government vessel to risk follow-ing us. Eventually they gave up, and we arrived, unmolested, back in Strood at around 2 AM the following morning. It had been a long jour-ney out and back, and I would have to be in work in just a few hours' time, but I was elated as I drove home.

As it turned out, we were the last people to be chased during that particular government campaign: just a few days later, the DTI, con-cerned at the massive cost of keeping a fully staffed surveillance ship at sea throughout the winter, and with Radio Caroline obviously not about to capitulate as Laser had done, ended their campaign, and reverted to their former tactic of occasional monitoring of ports to try to intercept boats and supplies. Although they had got Laser 558 off the air, they were a bit miffed that Caroline had immediately taken over the vacant 558 Khz channel, which gave a better signal than the one they had formerly used.

In the months that followed, I couldn't shake the memory of the visit out of my mind, and I found myself thinking more and more about what it must be like to live and work out at sea. Many of Caro-line's supporters harboured desires to go and work for the station, but few ever got the chance to do so, as joining the station meant giving up both your employment and your home, and spending long spells out at sea. Any sensible person would follow their example, and stay safely employed on land, content with being a listener. However, the romance and adventure of the enterprise had seized hold of me, and after a fair amount of thought over the following months, I finally de-cided to do something about it.

My ambition, however, was somewhat different from that of many of the people who wanted to go there. Despite my experience with South East Sound, I had little interest in being a DJ: I wanted to try for a position as newsreader. I'd always had a very keen interest in current affairs and world news and had thought about becoming a journalist when I left school, but the course I had wanted to do had been full, and I'd been sidetracked into the computer industry. I had done a certain amount of writing for various school and other magazines, and I felt that selecting and writing news stories – and reading them on air – would not be beyond me.

By this stage, through my friendship with John, I had come into contact with a few Caroline personnel. I mentioned my ambition to one of them, a DJ named Richard Jackson. Richard was extremely supportive and invited me to his house in Ashtead on a number of occasions. He sat patiently listening as I tried compiling and reading news bulletins from teletext; he coached and encouraged me, and did not allow me to make a tape until I had progressed from the level of completely useless to something approaching a promising amateur. Then he got me to make recording after recording until at last there was one he was satisfied with. He promised to bring it to the attention of the programme controller, Peter Phillips, when he went back out to the ship the following week. My boss, Tony Williams, was, as usual, very understanding, telling me that if I managed to get accepted on to Radio Caroline, my job with APS would still be waiting for me when I returned to land. In the meantime, I could carry on working for him while I tried to get on to Caroline.

Richard went back out to sea at the end of November 1986 and duly appeared on air, so I knew that the tape must have reached the ship. But as the weeks passed, and Christmas came and went, I guessed that my audition tape must have been deemed to be not good enough. A high turnover of staff meant that new people were always needed on board, especially in midwinter, so if I had sounded in any way decent, they would surely have contacted me immediately. I gradually pushed my dreams of joining Caroline as a newsreader to the back of my mind and, as the new year of 1987 rolled around, settled down again to my role as a computer engineer, installer and troubleshooter.

When Richard eventually returned to shore, it was with surprising news: my demo tape had never even reached the ship. There had been an accident when transferring supplies in November, and his bags had fallen into the sea, together with all his possessions. He seemed quite unperturbed by the incident, however, and his first thoughts on getting back on dry land was not to buy himself more clothes but to get another demo tape made for me!

Peter Phillips had also taken a break from the ship, and Richard arranged for me to meet him one evening at the Railway Tavern in

Surbiton. He seemed interested in what I had to say, and promised to listen to the demo tape and let me know. After that, though, I heard nothing, and once again my life carried along as usual. Again, it seemed as if my dreams would not be realised, and I tried to forget all about it.

Until one night, I got a phone call . . .

2

YES

FEBRUARY 1987–APRIL 1987FEBRUARY 1987–APRIL 1987

The call came at the worst possible time. It was a Sunday night, and I had been up for thirty-six hours straight, having been called out in the early hours of Sunday morning by John Burch to a fault in the Ensignbus computer system. Finally home at 10.30 PM, I was getting into bed for my long-awaited sleep. I actually had one leg in bed when my landlady knocked on my door. 'Phone,' she called. 'Some weird-sounding bloke called Cosmic.'

Tired as I was, my heart raced. Cosmic was from the inner sanctum of Caroline. He was a former crew member and now organised everything for the ship and acted as a liaison between those on board and Ronan O'Rahilly. I picked up the phone and introduced myself, listening with delighted disbelief as Cosmic (who sounded as way-out as his name implied) told me that my demo tape had been heard and approved by the station management, and that the job of newsreader on the station was mine if I wanted it.

Mine if I wanted it! A delicious sense of excitement mixed with fear washed over me. It was all very well dreaming of going to work for Caroline, but now I would have to make a decision between the safe and the unknown. The dream was mine for the taking. If I wanted it.

I wanted it.

Then came an even bigger shock. Cosmic explained to me that, due to a mix-up, I had not been contacted when I should have been,

19

and that they wanted me to go out to the ship on a supply boat that would be leaving quite soon.

'How soon?' I asked.

'Tonight. If you want the job, you've got to be ready to be picked up in two hours' time. Are you on?'

I hesitated for a fraction of a second, as it came home to me that my next word would determine my path in life. I weighed up the options. I could see this chance of a lifetime disappearing if I said that I needed more time. Would I ever get another one? It was about time I did something wild and adventurous.

I took a deep breath and said, 'Yes'.

'That's great, man,' Cosmic said, going on to tell me that I should bring only bare essentials, mostly clothes. He also told me to bring an ample supply of any medicines or toiletries I might need, as supply boats visited Caroline only once a fortnight and, other than that, there was no contact or way of getting hold of things you might need.

'You've gotta realise, man, once you're out there, you're out there,' he advised. Cosmic said he would come by and pick me up sometime around 1 AM. I didn't want him waking my flatmates, and I would have to bring the company van back to the office before I left anyway, so I arranged that we would meet on the forecourt of Surbiton train station. I looked at my watch: two hours and fifteen minutes to tie up the loose ends of my old life before embarking on the new one.

All trace of fatigue gone, I paced the hallway for a few moments, thinking about what I had just done and what I had to do before I left. I knew that once I was eighteen miles out at sea, there would be no chance of rectifying any omission. I dialled Tony's home number, hoping to be able to apologise for the fact that I was leaving my job so quickly that I wouldn't even see him in the morning. He was out, and I had to leave the message with his babysitter. I then went to see my landlady, explained where I was going and wrote out a cheque to her for eight weeks' rent, knowing that I would be gone for a minimum of six weeks. I packed quickly, then headed in to the office.

Letting myself in to the small shop on Brighton Road, I could hardly believe how much was about to change as the result of one phone call. Everything in the office was just as I had left it on Friday evening, but now Monday morning would see me far away from the little computer shop beside the Total petrol station on Brighton Road.

I just made it to Surbiton station by 1 AM, listening on the car radio to Caroline closing down for the night, thinking that within a few short hours I would be out there myself. Time passed, and there was no sign of Cosmic. Eventually it got so late that I thought he had missed me, or changed his plans, but he finally showed up at 2:30, driving his battered Volvo incredibly fast. He apologised for being late, then followed as I drove the half-mile or so back to APS to leave the company vehicle in the car park for the final time.

Once in the Volvo, I was introduced to Tim Shepherd, who was joining Caroline as a new DJ, and was then told that our next stop was Ashtead, to pick up Richard, who was going out for another stint with us. I relaxed a bit: at least I would have one friend on board.

Cosmic may have been a stereotypical hippie, but there was nothing gentle about his driving. After picking up Richard, we raced down the motorway at incredible speed, as Richard explained that poor time-keeping, manic driving and battered Volvos were the trademark of Caroline's land organisation. We got to Dover just in time to miss the 4 AM ferry; while sitting in the café waiting for the next one, Cosmic and Richard explained to Tim and me, as newcomers, exactly what the plans were for the trip out to Caroline, and about the legalities surrounding our trip.

At this time, Caroline was broadcasting on two radio frequencies: one, in English, on 558 KHz medium wave as Caroline, and one on 963 KHz; this frequency was rented out to a Dutch pirate station during the day and to American religious broadcasters by night. The Dutch service paid its rent by providing all the fuel oil, food and water necessary to keep the ship and its transmitters running, and arranged the bi-weekly supply boats which went out from France. This was a good arrangement for Caroline, as it meant that nothing was done directly from the UK and no laws were broken: the French authorities turned a blind eye to the supply boats (or 'tenders') leaving their ports. In theory, British people working for Caroline would be breaking the law – though that did not affect me as an Irish citizen. However, the chances of our being stopped leaving the country among all the regular ferry passengers were slim. Cosmic told us that the British government did show occasional surges of interest, with DTI officers stationed at ports to look for Caroline staff going to and from the Continent. Usually nothing much came of these, but we would have to be careful going through Customs, just in case. As the kind of person who always feels guilty going through Customs, even when I have nothing to hide, I wondered how good I would be at hiding my intentions now that I was actually engaged in something illicit. There was no going back, though: I wanted this too much to let a minor worry get in the way.

Cosmic also talked to me about pay – something which had not been discussed in our earlier phone call. I knew from the stories that John Burch passed on to me that pay for working on Caroline could be highly variable, and occasionally nonexistent, with people tending to get what they needed to survive rather than being paid huge wages. Richard joined Cosmic in reassuring me that, with the station currently running well, everyone was getting paid at the end of their stints, the exact amount depending on how long you had been with the station and any particular needs you might have. While out on board the *Ross Revenge*, we would be living very cheaply, as we would be fed and looked after, and not able to spend any money.

By the time we had finished this chat, it was time for us to board our ferry. The four of us remained anxiously silent as we drove from the main booking hall along the road that led towards the ships – and Customs. Luckily, we passed through Customs without even being asked our names – although Cosmic then managed to turn even the short drive up the ramp into the ferry into a test of speed and skill, ignoring the fact that we were meant not to be drawing attention to ourselves.

When we arrived in Calais, Cosmic told us that the tender was due to leave Dunkirk – ten miles or so away – in just forty-five minutes. Cue some more speedy driving, during which he nearly ran at least two cars off the road. In Dunkirk, we bumped along a cobbled quayside, where we found the Dutch supply tender *Bellatrix*, which, contrary to our expectations of an imminent departure, was devoid of any sign of life. Cosmic flew into a rage, calling the Dutch all the names under the sun. We withdrew to a local café, where he phoned the tender's Belgian skipper, Willie, and found out that it was, in fact, scheduled to depart at 9 PM rather than AM.

Thankfully, when we returned to the *Bellatrix* at about midday, it was unlocked, and Cosmic and Richard showed Tim and me to some cabins, where I at once dived straight into bed. As I drifted off to sleep in the dark cabin, I thought of my colleges at APS, who would now be halfway through their normal Monday chores, doubtless tutting and shaking their heads at my abrupt departure. As I thought about the fact that I was about to cut myself off from civilisation, to a place where all the skills I had learned since leaving school would be useless. I drifted into an uneasy sleep.

When I awoke, vibrations and sounds of life came at me from every direction. The sounds were unfamiliar and, as I regained consciousness, the now-familiar mixture of delight and fear washed over me again. I made my way upstairs to deck level, to see that we had just pulled away from the quayside. The *Bellatrix* seemed to be swarming with Dutchmen, who turned out to be crew for the Dutch service Radio Monique, on their way out to relieve their comrades on board the *Ross* who were due shore leave. Freddie Bolland was also there. Bolland, a large, jovial man, was the owner of Monique and handled all the money that was paid for fuel and supplies to the ship. Listening to Caroline on 558, you only heard English staff, and would never guess that almost all of the station's important business was transacted through France and Holland. The Dutch station Radio Monique was as popular in Holland and Belgium as Caroline was in England, and different laws over there allowed it to carry a great deal of advertising – hence its financial importance to the whole setup.

One of the Dutch going out introduced himself as Erwin Van Der Bliek, a Monique DJ. He chatted away to me, explaining what I would find when I finally got out to the Caroline ship. As we talked, the *Bellatrix* cleared the last of the harbour gates and slipped out to sea, Dunkirk dwindling to a long strip of orange light behind us.

It was almost 4 AM when we approached the Caroline ship, and I went out on deck to watch. It was more than a year since my earlier, brief visit to the ship; now I would get to know it very intimately indeed.

The *Ross Revenge* was a cluster of lights in the darkness, and, as we got closer, I began to see just how huge she was. The *Bellatrix* slowed, and Willie nudged her bow directly up to the stern of the *Ross*. There was a clang and a jolt as the two ships met, and then a burst of furious activity as Dutchmen rushed all over the place, shouting, and throwing and catching ropes to tie the vessels together. They then manhandled between the ships two great big plastic pipelines which would pump thousands of gallons of diesel oil and fresh water from the *Bellatrix* to the radio ship. I stood quietly out of the way on the front deck of the tender, waiting for the signal to step across on to the other ship.

The arrival of the supply vessel was obviously a big event for the Caroline crew, and more and more sleepy-eyed people appeared out on the back deck of the *Ross* to see what – and who – it had brought them. There was some annoyance when it was discovered that there were only two English DJs on the *Bellatrix*, as apparently four people wanted to get off for a break. Kevin Turner, the acting programme controller of Caroline, seemed particularly annoyed, but he was pleased to hear that I was joining them as a newsreader, as apparently there had not been one for a while, and the DJs had had to do extra shifts to cover the news.

Willie eventually beckoned us right up to the front, where we waited as the two ships moved up and down against each other until we stepped across. I breathed a sigh or relief when I was standing firmly on the *Ross Revenge*: compared to the bobbing of the *Bellatrix*, it seemed as solid as a rock. Following the others, I climbed down a ladder from the back deck of the *Ross*, went through a small metal doorway leading to the inside of the vessel and located the mess room, where incoming and outgoing staff were meeting briefly to swap gossip before they parted ways.

It was a scene of absolute bedlam, with people rushing round everywhere, and paying no attention to Tim or me; we just sat in a corner and watched. Cosmic was rushing around with manic energy, checking that all was well on board the ship, making sure that he would be able to give Ronan O'Rahilly a comprehensive report about the status of the operation when he returned to land with the tender. Meanwhile, the ship's Alsatian dog, Raffles, a permanent resident, was running around, getting under everyone's feet, and generally looking for any opportunity to swipe some of the food that had come on board. A tall Dutchman emerged from the crowd and bore down on us, giving us a warm handshake and speaking in perfect English.

'Hi, I'm Ad Roberts, the programme controller of Monique – I know everyone's fairly busy when there's a tender alongside and tend to neglect the new arrivals, but I just want you to know that you're very welcome aboard.'

A long blast of a ship's horn from outside told us that the *Bellatrix* was getting ready to go. There was a sudden rush for the back deck by the departing crew, most of whom I hadn't even met, and no sooner had they scrambled on to the *Bellatrix* than the ropes were cast off. She circled us slowly once, giving another long blast on her horn, before turning and heading away into the night. Her lights dwindled in the distance and went out of sight altogether, and we were alone on the dark sea.

Now I was past the point of no return. Here I was, eighteen miles from the nearest land, and with no chance of backing out gracefully when the time came to go on air. What was it Cosmic had said? 'You've gotta realise, man, once you're out there, you're out there.'

Oh, I realised it all right.

Comparative calm descended on the *Ross Revenge*, and I sought out Kevin Turner, who was to be my boss, to ask him when he wanted me to start. I expected him to tell me to get some sleep, and possibly familiarise myself with the newsroom later on before starting duties the following day, but he pushed me straight in at the deep end, telling me to start work at 6.30 AM, with the first headlines of the day.

The equipment in the newsroom consisted of a very old and battered typewriter, a broken chair, and a teletext TV. A microphone jutted out over the desk, and there was a pair of headphones. I would have to listen out for when the DJ fired the news jingle, the end of which would be my cue to speak. A large red light over the TV would indicate when I was live, the mike being controlled from the studio downstairs. Kevin gave me a few tips about what was expected of me, then went downstairs to prepare for his programme. I was nervous, but I had to start sometime, I told myself, and quickly dialled up BBC news on the teletext, to see what I could report on. The clock ticked away towards 6.30 as I struggled to cope with the ancient typewriter, which felt like lead in my hands compared to the computer keyboards I was used to. It was 24 February 1987, and Steve Conway, newsreader, was about to be born before about 3 million listeners on the breakfast show.

I had expected to be poor at first and to gain in confidence as the day went on, but I had completely overestimated my ability: that first news-shift was a disaster. The two lines of headlines at 6.30 went OK, but the full news at 7 AM was a different matter. I had only managed to compile four stories, despite hammering away on the typewriter for all I was worth, and I read them terribly, stumbling through them with words wrongly emphasised and pauses in all the wrong places. At the end of the bulletin, I almost forgot to give Kevin my out-cue: 'For Caroline 558, this is Steve Conway.' I didn't dare imagine what Kevin must have been thinking.

I went down one level to the studio, knocked and entered. 'I'm really sorry about that, Kevin, I know I wasn't very good, but I just need a little practice. I'll be much better on the next one, I promise.'

Kevin stared at the wall for a long minute, and seemed to be trying very hard to keep his patience. Eventually, he stared at me. 'Fine,' he said. 'If you want to do something useful, go down to the galley and make me a cup of tea.'

I scrambled out of the studio, grateful to escape an ear-bashing, and praying that he wasn't thinking of taking me off the air and sending me home in disgrace. Luckily, my next main news bulletin, at 8 AM, did indeed show some signs of improvement, although it still fell far short of the quality usually found on Caroline. Kevin didn't make any further comment to me, and after the 9 AM news, my first shift was over.

As Caroline only had news at peak times, I would next read at 1 PM, and then do the evening news shift, with bulletins at 4, 5 and 6. I made up my mind to start work on these at least an hour and a half in advance, as I clearly needed to put in a lot of work. Kevin was off air at 9 AM, and Richard was on for the next four hours. Everyone else seemed to be in bed, so I decided to unwind by exploring my new surroundings. I started by looking around the top level, where the newsroom was, and working my way down.

Level after level of the ship yielded long corridors, doorways galore, and many empty rooms. On the top level, there was the bridge, a large, curved room full of navigation equipment, with a beautiful brass-plated compass taking pride of place in the centre. Off that was the newsroom, which itself provided access through another doorway to a cabin, where the resident ship's engineers lived. (Apparently they slept all day and worked at night.) Two doors at either end gave access to balconies outside, and there were steps down to the back deck, where I had arrived earlier. A very steep staircase went down into the ship to the next level, where the Caroline 558 and Monique 963 studios sat side by side, separated by a glass partition. Compared to the newsroom, these were well equipped, bristling with turntables, cartridge machines, mixers, speakers and other electronic equipment. Across from them was the record library, an airy and sumptuous room lined with row after row of albums and singles – some ten thousand in all. Also on this level was a toilet and shower room.

Going down another almost-vertical stairway, I came to the main deck level of the ship, where a long metal corridor ran straight for some distance, with doorways on either side, then curved around, before forking into two, one way going to the very back of the ship, the other out to the main port-side deck. Off this corridor there were doorways leading to the outside and to various rooms, including the galley, a large, tiled room with gas cookers and an enormous sink and draining-board unit. The mess room, with its long table, swivel chairs and television, was also along this corridor, as was the Dutch newsroom – little more than a cubbyhole – more toilets, a shower and washroom, and the food stores at the very back, directly under the back deck. Also off this corridor were various deserted rooms, some full of dusty machinery, and the engine room, where level after level of metal catwalks led down past a monstrously big engine to dark alleyways full of mechanical and electrical equipment which was rarely used. (The ship stayed at its anchorage under all conditions, barring the occasional broken anchor chain.)

Outside, the port and starboard deck joined in the middle of the ship to form the main deck, out of which came the radio tower. At three hundred feet, it was the tallest mast which had ever been mounted on a ship, and just looking up at it made you feel dizzy. Stays (guy wires) led from it to every conceivable point on the ship, and in the middle of its base was a huge ceramic insulator, the size of a tall gatepost, where the high-voltage aerial cables passed through the deck from the transmitter room directly underneath. The transmitter room, reached by a long metal stairs through a hatch off the main deck, housed three large medium-wave transmitters: one for 558, one for 963, and one spare. This area was off-limits to all but the engineers, as was the generator room next to it, where MAN diesel engines thundered away twenty-four hours a day, providing the ship with the hundreds of kilowatts of electricity needed for the transmitters, as well as the light and heat for the rest of the ship. At the very front of the ship, you could climb up on to the bow, where an anchor chain with links of eight-inch-thick steel dropped into the sea, holding the ship in its position year in, year out.

The view was of unbroken sea in all directions but one, where a small red blob could be seen: Caroline's friend, rival and competitor, the *MV Communicator*, home of Laser radio, now back out at sea and broadcasting on 576 medium wave.

Erwin, the Dutch DJ I had met on the journey out the previous night, joined me on deck, and gave me some details about our location, and the landmarks, or lack of them, on the horizon. This far out at sea, land could not be seen, and there were no passing ships, only the *Communicator* in the distance, fixed in position, as we were. Every six hours, the *Ross Revenge* would swing around with the changing tide to point in the opposite direction, though this was hard to notice, in the absence of any landmarks. Our anchorage was off the Essex coast, at a place called the Knock Deep. According to Erwin, the sandbanks about half a mile away on either side of us broke the waves and meant that the sea never got too rough in anything other than a north-easterly wind, our one unprotected direction.

By the time I had explored most of the ship, it was time for the lunchtime news. The evening news quickly followed, and I finished up at six having done some not particularly good bulletins during the *Drivetime* show.

Straight after six, it was down to the mess room for dinner. I was told that this was the main social event of the day, the one time that everybody got together. I took a seat on the outside of the table, at the end nearest the door, feeling very nervous in front of all these new people, who must surely have been discussing my dreadful performance before I came into the room. There were ten of us in all: three Dutch DJs, five English DJs, the engineer and myself. Richard introduced me to everyone, including Peter Chicago, the chief engineer and something of a living legend amongst staff past and present.

Peter, tall and strong, and with a dry sarcastic sense of humour, had worked for Caroline for seventeen years, on both the *Ross Revenge* and the *Mi Amigo*. If rumour was to be believed, Chicago was a very difficult man to get on with, and if he didn't like you, you tended not to get asked back out for a second stint. I had already decided to stay well out of his way, and was glad that he had been fast asleep earlier, when I had been performing so badly. Caroline's longest-serving employee would surely not have approved of a rank amateur like me. Keen to redeem myself in Kevin's and Chicago's eyes, I volunteered to do the washing up that night. I filled a large cauldron with water and put it on to boil, under the watchful eye of Chicago, who then proceeded to tear strips off me. Apparently there were two taps in the galley, one for fresh water (which was jealously hoarded) and another with salt water taken straight from the sea. I had committed the cardinal sin of using fresh water for the washing up, and Chicago made sure I understood how wasteful I had been, leaving me feeling wretched. My first day on board, and apart from upsetting the programme controller and staff with my dreadful newsreading, I had now fallen foul of the chief engineer too.

At this stage, I just wanted to go to bed, as I had been up for so long, and also because my newsroom duties entailed a 5 AM start on weekday mornings. Erwin showed me to a dark stairway that led off the main corridor down to below the waterline – and to an utterly tranquil, softly lit passageway, with numbered doorways along either side. He gave me Cabin Four, which had been vacated by one of the departing crew, and I lugged my rucksack down from the mess room and closed the door behind me.

The cabin was very nice: quiet and peaceful, with a bunk set high up into the wall, and a bench, table, wardrobe and washbasin. A speaker high up on the wall relayed the radio station, and could be turned on or off as required. The bunk was coffin-like, and almost completely enclosed – to prevent the occupant falling out during rough weather – but it was very comfortable and I put out the light and, despite my anxieties about the events of the day, was quickly lulled into a deep sleep by the waves gently lapping at the hull outside.

Kevin woke me, as arranged, just after 5 AM the next morning, and I struggled out of the bunk and climbed down on to the floor. By 5.30, I was washed, dressed and up in the newsroom with a cup of tea, ready to start the day's work. The first task was to listen to the shipping forecast on Radio 4, to help with compiling weather reports, and to notify the crew of any impending severe weather conditions. A shipping forecast could also be had on ITV teletext but, according to everyone on board, the Radio 4 one was much more accurate. I also had to prepare a weather report to be read each hour by the on-air DJ, which included local wind, sea and visibility conditions, as an aid to the many coastal fishermen who tuned into Caroline each day before putting out to sea. For this, I had to go out on deck, observe the sea, check if I could see as far as the *Communicator* and a nearby navigation beacon, and judge the wind strength, before checking the wind direction against the compass on the bridge. At the same time, I was typing out the first of the day's travel-news reports, and scanning the teletext for important news stories from around the world to cover in my bulletins.

At least this time I knew better what was involved, and by the time 7 AM came around, I had six good stories typed out and ready. I had also practised them beforehand, so there were not so many slip-ups. I was still reasonably bad, and also tended to 'pop' the microphone a lot. (My 'P's and 'B's made little popping sounds.) However, Kevin could see that I was making an effort and was friendlier towards me as I brought him the numerous cups of tea he required. He talked about the pay on Caroline: 'Not a lot at first, but more if you come back for a second stint. The old man's sick of one-trip wonders and tends to pay for loyalty.' He also told me how the secret of Caroline's success in the 1980s lay in the design of its extra-strong broadcast tower, which had stood for four years through all sorts of weather, while Laser had lost about four or five masts. 'If it ever does come down,' he said, gesturing upwards, 'that'll be the end of us – the Dutch will pull out straight away and we'll be broke within weeks.'

As part of my news duties, I also had to read a bulletin on the Dutch service Radio Monique, who had international news (in English) at 8.25 AM, and again at 3.30 PM. This made me somewhat unique on board: the English DJs only broadcast on Caroline 558, and the Dutch were confined to Monique on 963; I was the only voice that was heard on both. The Dutch newsroom, which was just opposite the mess room, was no bigger than a broom-cupboard. When I went in there, twice a day, the Dutch newsreader had to go out, as there just wasn't room for both of us.

I soon fell into the pattern of life on the ship, and although I had a reasonable amount of spare time in those first few days, I was never bored. Richard gave me extra tuition to help me with my newsreading whenever he could. The atmosphere on the ship was very relaxed. As well as the music playing softly from speakers in every room, there was the record library, with its thousands of titles. The library had a record player and was a popular gathering place on board for listening to music, reading something from the good selection of books or just socialising. I continued exploring the ship, and there was always someone around to talk to. The beauty of the *Ross Revenge* was that, as a ship built for a crew of fifty back in its days as a trawler, it held a crew of ten very comfortably indeed. There were plenty of empty places to wander around on my own if I felt like it.

Erwin was a great help to me in my early days on board, despite the fact that his own on-air duties on the Dutch service kept him tied up for most of the day. Aged twenty, a couple of years younger than me, he was bristling with enthusiasm and obviously regarded his job as a Monique DJ as a wonderful opportunity. He had been on the station for more than a year and must have come across countless new inexperienced Caroline crew in that time, but he always made the time to chat or give me tips.

The first weekend came, and I was fascinated to notice that, although one day at sea was much like another, there was still a very different feel about Saturday on the ship. People did their programmes at different times, to give the early DJs a lie-in at the weekend, and although I still had to get up before 6 AM for the news, the schedule was not so intensive, and the day felt more relaxed. Richard was on weekend breakfast, and it was nice to work as the newsreader during his programme. Chicago was making an effort to be friendly to me after our initial run-in, and he dug out an old pop-shield for the news mike, thereby curing one of my worst problems. After my shaky start, I was definitely beginning to get the hang of things.

In the early hours of Sunday morning, my sleep was shattered by the clanging of alarm bells ringing throughout the ship. I was excited: I had read the notices and knew that one long ring on the alarm bell meant that we had a tender. I wondered who, or what, it might have brought us.

I struggled into my clothes and upstairs, to find that it was just after 3 AM and bitterly cold out on deck. A small fishing boat was tied up on our starboard side, and various people were climbing aboard the *Ross*. The boat had, it seemed, been sent out directly from England (a very rare occurrence) to bring out the replacements for the two people who hadn't been able to leave with the *Bellatrix*. Kevin Turner and Jamie King were going, and three people were coming on. One, a seasoned Caroline DJ, Mark Matthews, was to stand in as programme controller, while the two others were a new DJ and a cook.

Remembering how I had felt when I had arrived just a few days earlier, I wandered over to speak to the newcomers, an Australian DJ called Mark Warner and the new cook, Penny. I found them both vacant cabins and showed them some of the living arrangements on board.

With some people having left and others having arrived, the programme schedules had all changed, but my working day was the same as usual and I concentrated on trying to improve my newsreading. Richard offered to cook dinner that night so that Penny could have a long sleep, and he came up with a nice meal. It was strange to sit around the table with some people missing and others having replaced them. And it was certainly strange that some people were even newer to the ship than me!

Mark Matthews's style, both as a leader and as a DJ, was to prove very different to Kevin's, and dawn on Monday morning saw the start of a partnership on the breakfast programme between presenter and newsreader which was to grow into something quite enjoyable. After the news headlines, which came at half past each hour in the morning, Mark would chat to me on air, with me as the straight guy to his often very devious sense of humour. The bulk of his programme was very entertaining. The music, of course, was the same whatever the presenter (Caroline ran to a strict format as far as the music went) but Mark somehow seemed able to bring lots of verve and sparkle to the show. The interplay between DJ and newsreader became gradually more daring as the days went on, and all the time I was gaining in confidence.

One night after dinner, Mark Matthews called me aside and took me up to the record library for a private chat. I expected it to be an assessment of how I was doing – or perhaps a suggestion for some new antics for the breakfast show – but he floored me with a completely unexpected request: he wanted me to do some programmes as a DJ.

Mark explained that Caroline tried to run twenty-four hours a day whenever possible, but that there were not enough staff to do so at the moment. He knew that my newsroom duties occupied me all day long, especially during the week, but asked if I would like to do an overnight programme at the weekends so that Caroline could pick up listeners among the large number of people who were out and about during the night on Friday and Saturday. He said he would get someone to cover the lunchtime news on Saturday and Sunday so that I could sleep in the middle of the day. Although I was pleased to be asked, I turned him down, explaining that I had always wanted to do the news, and that, despite my love of music, I thought I just didn't have what it took to become a DJ. Mark was quite surprised by my response: apparently I was the first person who had ever turned down the chance to do a show!

Mark asked me again on the Thursday night before my second weekend on board, but again I turned him down, happy to stay working in the newsroom, which by this time I felt I could handle. On the Friday morning at about a quarter to six, as I was starting my morning shift, Chicago cornered me in the newsroom, which he passed through every morning on his way to bed. Towering over me, he explained how anxious he was for Caroline to get as large an audience as possible, and how important it was that the station was on through the night at weekends. 'Mark tells me he thinks you would be quite capable of doing an overnight programme at weekends,' he said. 'Can I count on you to help us out?' With the request coming from Chicago, and sounding more like a command than a request, I didn't feel that I could refuse.

Mark was jubilant when I told him I had decided to do it, and said that he'd talk to me later in the day about what it entailed. 'So Chicago had the same idea as me, then. Funny old world, isn't it?' he said with a grin, leaving me in no doubt about who had put Chicago up to it.

I worked through the rest of my morning news shift with a certain amount of dread, coupled with excitement. Finally 9 AM came, and Mark took me into the record library and sat me down to discuss what I would be doing. I was down to present the 1 to 5 AM programme on the Friday, Saturday and Sunday nights (or rather the early hours of Saturday, Sunday and Monday mornings).

Caroline's music format meant that all the music was chosen for me: current hits and new record plays were rotated on a card-index system in the studio, and oldies on a printed list produced from a much bigger and more slowly rotating system. The current records would be in the studio already, and the oldies list would have the record filing number against each title, so that they could be easily pulled from the library. There was also a set of presentation guidelines; these gave advice about the how the format worked, what to say and what not to say, and how the adverts rotated. (Caroline had one major advertiser at this point: the Canadian National Lottery Lotto 6/49.)

Some people had criticised the format in the past, but it gave the station a uniform sound and helped new DJs blend in. Before the station was formatted by Peter Phillips in 1985, anyone could play whatever they wanted to. This sounded fine in theory but, in practice, although some DJs produced brilliant shows, others were less consistent, and every time there was a tender and the crew changed, the whole sound of the station altered, and listeners drifted away. Now, Caroline still played a much broader range of pop and rock than other stations, but in a consistent way.

The rest of the day flew by and, before long, it was dinnertime, with the evening, and my first night's performance, rushing towards me. Tim Shepherd, who did the late-night programme leading up to mine, said he would wake me at 11 PM and show me how the studio worked; he would also be around during the night if I needed help. I went to bed after dinner to get a few hours' sleep, knowing that I wouldn't be seeing much of my bed until Monday. As I was drifting off to sleep with the cabin speaker softly relaying Caroline, I was surprised to hear the news jingle, followed by the voice of Mark Matthews reading a newsflash. I listened intently as he read out initial reports about a ferry which had capsized in Zeebrugge harbour, with many people on board.

In the end, I didn't get much sleep, and was up before Tim came to wake me, pulling my classic tracks from the library. I took Tim in a cup of coffee, and he showed me how to operate the big old-fashioned mixer. It was nothing like the sort of mixer you usually see in radio station or discos, or the sort I had used before on South East Sound – it was all controlled by knobs rather than sliding faders – but I soon got to grips with it. There were two record decks to one side, three cart machines, which could be used to play adverts, jingles and some pre-carted music, and, of course, a microphone. All the items had remote-start buttons directly in front of the DJ, so you didn't have to reach halfway round the room to start something off. The studio itself had a lovely warm cosy feel, and two windows gave an excellent view out over the sea and the back deck – although at this time of night there was little to see. Soon 1 AM came around, and Tim put on his last record and left the studio to me, promising to bring me a cup of tea at some stage. I cued up my first record according to the format ('When a Man Loves a Woman' by Percy Sledge) and watched the seconds tick away as Tim's record drew to a close. I steeled myself for my first announcement, the standard Caroline top-of-the-hour speech-with-bell jingle, and pressed start on Percy Sledge, opening the mike at the same time. 'On 558 kilohertz, this is Radio Caroline,' I began, and pressed another button for the 'ding ding' of the bell.

Percy started singing, and I realised with horror that I had put him on at the wrong speed: 33 RPM instead of 45. I quickly corrected the mistake and sat back in shame, shot down in flames before my programme had even taken off. Oh well, things could only get better.

I introduced myself over the start of the second record (the Eurthymics' 'Thorn in My Side') and after that spoke after every third or fourth record, concentrating mainly on getting the hang of the equipment, so that the record starts and stops would be smooth and tight. It seemed very strange to be sitting in the 558 studio playing records that, in some cases, had come into the current rotation while I was still on shore – songs I had listened to on Caroline as I drove around southwest London in my APS van. It was quite fun once I got the hang of it, although the speech element still needed a lot of thought: I was used to being a serious-sounding newsreader and just couldn't think of what to say when I spoke every fifteen minutes or so.

At about 3 AM, there was a scratching and bumping against the studio door. I opened the door, and Raffles bounded in. Everyone else on the ship had gone to bed, and he wanted company. He lay down

quietly at my feet and was as good as gold during the rest of the programme. The hours stretched long through the night, but finally it was
5 AM, and Mark Warner came in to do the weekend breakfast show.

Now, according to the agreement with Mark Matthews, I should
have been able to go to bed at 9 AM and sleep till 3, but because of the
ferry disaster the previous night, I judged that there would have to be
extra bulletins during the day, and that I would stay up to handle them.
There was a grim mood on the *Ross Revenge* that Saturday as the full
death toll from the *Herald of Free Enterprise* became apparent. It was
hard to believe that such a large ship, professionally maintained and
crewed, could come to grief so easily. That, and the fact that the Zeebrugge route was sometimes used by Caroline staff going to the Continent (to draw attention away from our use of Dover), brought home
to us that we were only ever guests on the sea, and not a fixed part of
it. Although no lives had been lost when the *Mi Amigo* had broken anchor, run aground and sunk seven years before, that too could have
easily turned into a tragedy.

I manned the newsroom right through the day, producing extra
bulletins as the enormity of the Zeebrugge tragedy became apparent.
By the time the evening came, I was almost too tired to eat, and was
glad to slip down to my cabin for a few hours' sleep. The weekend
dragged by slowly, and on Monday I gratefully settled back into my
normal routine of news only.

During the next week, I encountered my first stormy weather on
board the ship, when a north-westerly wind turned the sea white-
streaked with foam and I could feel the *Ross* move under me for the
first time. As Erwin had said, the Knock Deep was an excellent anchorage: although the winds were quite strong, the sandbanks broke
the force of the swell, and the ship merely moved from side to side
very slowly, never going over too far. The only time it rocked with anything other than a gentle motion was when it turned with the tide and
the waves caught it on the side.

After a couple of days of stormy weather, the sea returned to a
calm state. The time flew by as I settled into life on board the ship,
feeling that I had found my own niche in the little community. One
calm April evening, the *Bellatrix* arrived, bringing with it Peter Phillips

– the top dog in Caroline's shipboard pecking order. I was a bit anxious when Peter arrived, as he was known to be a stickler, and as the programme controller he could easily have had me sent home if he didn't like my news style. However, by this stage I was a passable newsreader, and he was happy to let me stay. He told me that, as a DJ, I needed to make a lot of effort to improve my style, but added kindly that at least I wasn't as bad at it as some people who'd been out on the ship in the past.

On the *Bellatrix* with Peter was Mike Watts, a relief engineer, so Chicago was able to go home to his wife for a few weeks – much to the disappointment of Raffles, who stood on deck looking out to sea and pining for days afterwards. Raffles was used to Chicago going ashore by this stage, but it didn't stop him from missing him. In fact, any time someone mentioned the word 'tender', the dog would rush outside in a state of great excitement and scan the horizon for any ships that might be bringing his master 'home'.

Also joining us was Tom Anderson, one of the longest-standing Caroline presenters. Tom had started his career in radio on the *Mi Amigo* and had been one of the three people rescued from the ship the night it sank. He then became the first person to broadcast on the *Ross Revenge*, in 1983, and had been a regular crew member ever since.

Now, however, he was here for his last-ever stint out at sea with Caroline, having decided to retire from the station to pursue a more normal life, and he was really only on board to gather up his belongings and some of his own personal records, and bring them ashore. Tom had a great sense of humour, and with both him and Mark Matthews on board, practical jokes became a way of life. Mark and I had played the odd trick on each other in the breakfast show, but now the three of us teamed up to plan a serious attempt to make life interesting for our Australian DJ, Mark Warner.

Warner's great conversation point was the fact that he had been on the Israeli pirate, The Voice of Peace, and he was forever telling us how much better than Caroline it was. Everything there had been absolutely perfect, according to him. After almost six weeks of hearing this, we were all getting pretty tired of it, and everyone cooperated in planning a morning's 'entertainment' for him.

We decided to tackle him on a Saturday morning, when he would be on weekend breakfast and all three plotters would have a legitimate excuse to be up and about: me because I would just finished my overnight shift; Tom because he was pretending that he was going to do the morning news shift to let me get extra sleep; and Mark Matthews because he was nocturnal anyway. Tom had been working on refurbishing the record library, thinning out albums and singles which were unsuitable for airplay, so we would have room to expand. He got together a collection of records which were cracked or chipped and too badly damaged to play, and which were about to be chucked. We pulverised these with a hammer, and the pieces were carefully inserted into the sleeves and covers of the albums and singles that were on the playlist for Warner's programme that morning; we hid the proper records carefully away. He had pulled his selection of records the previous night, so it was easy to replace them all and leave his pile looking exactly as he had left it.

Warner started his programme, and Mark, Tom and I sat in the record library pretending to be chatting innocently. After a few moments, Warner discovered the first record and came rushing out. 'Look at this – bloody thing's in pieces, you really should take more care of your records, you know – this would never happen on the *Peace* ship.' He grabbed another record and went back into the studio. A few moments later, we heard a muffled cry of rage from the direction of the studio, followed by another, and another. We got the real records out, left them outside the studio door, and fled upstairs to the newsroom laughing. From down below, we could hear the sound of slamming doors and stomping.

The broken records, however, were only the first part of our little plan that morning – as Warner found out when it came to newstime.

The seven o'clock news was read, with me, Mark and Tom each reading a story in turn – which in itself was unusual enough. However, instead of the usual five or six stories, we ran about twenty. We started off with genuine ones, and gradually made them sillier and sillier. As each story went by and the clock ticked the minutes away, Warner, downstairs in the studio, must have been desperately wondering when it would end. We eventually finished and let him get back to

39

his programme. He never said a word to us: he didn't even come out of the studio.

Our grand finale was the eight o'clock news, which, considering what had happened an hour earlier, Warner must have been dreading. The eight o'clock news featured the usual six stories, all normal ones, but was read by Mark, Tom and me in chorus, like a Welsh male voice choir. At the end, we announced ourselves as Steve Condom, Moira Anderson and Marcia Matthews.

Needless to say, Warner was not his usual chirpy self that day, but everyone else on the boat thought it had been hilarious – as I'm sure did most of the listeners. Obviously, we normally ran Caroline in a serious way, and the news in particular was usually very formal, but we believed that the odd bit of humour and clowning around was all right, as long as it didn't happen too often.

Unknown to us, though, Kevin Turner and Ronan had been listening to that morning's entertainment on shore and were far from impressed. But with the ship being eighteen miles out at sea and completely cut off, there was not very much they could do about it.

At this stage, I had been out on the ship for seven weeks and had decided it was time to take a break on shore to sort things out and see where my future lay. I really enjoyed Caroline and life on the ship, but I knew that the real test of whether they liked me was if they would allow me back out for a second stint. People were rarely asked to leave the ship unless they were really obnoxious, but there were many people who did one stint and were not invited back. The only way for me to find out would be to go off and see what happened. Also, to be fair to Tony Williams and APS, I couldn't ask him to hold my job open forever, so it was definitely time to sort things out.

We were actually expecting a tender that weekend, but it was a bit choppy on the Saturday night, and nothing came. The sea calmed down on the Sunday afternoon, and at about 6 PM the *Bellatrix* was spotted heading towards us. I had been prepared for its arrival, but it still seemed strange to think that this time I would be leaving on it instead of watching it sail away. Because the sea was still a bit rough, the *Bellatrix* dropped anchor a quarter of a mile away and started transferring people and supplies in a rubber speedboat. This craft could safely come alongside the *Ross* when larger ones would be in danger of being smashed against us by the waves.

The first person to clamber on board from the speedboat was Kevin Turner, fresh from his holiday and literally puffed up with rage. He made a beeline for Mark Matthews and started berating him loudly about the previous day's escapade in Mark Warner's programme. Soon Tom joined forces with Mark, Peter Phillips got caught in the middle, and a huge shouting match was under way, with me standing on the sidelines feeling quite guilty, because although I'd been in it up to my neck, apparently I was too junior for Kevin to bother shouting at. Perhaps my chances of being allowed back were not so good after all.

All of this was taking place in the middle of the usual melee of tendering, complicated by the fact that quite a lot of people were leaving and arriving, and the use of the rubber boat made getting on and off difficult.

Eventually the row subsided, and Tom reassured me that everything would blow over in a week or so. Darkness fell in the Knock Deep, and finally, at about 10 PM, it was time for those of us leaving to go in twos across to the *Bellatrix* in the rubber boat. It was nerve-racking to climb down into the little craft, which bounced around like a cork on the sea, while the *Ross* towered over us, firm and immovable. As we shot off across the water, I couldn't help but feel a tremendous surge of affection for the ship that had been my home these past few weeks. Its twinkling lights were reflected in the water, and it looked peaceful and pretty sitting there in a little pool of its own light.

We arrived back in Dunkirk early the following morning. I stood for a little while on the quayside, unused to the sights and sounds around me, before getting into Willie's car. I had stood on that same patch of quayside seven weeks before, but it seemed like a lifetime ago. I felt like a different person, and knew then that I would not be returning to APS. I might spend a couple of weeks or more on land, sorting out my ex-job and other aspects of my old life, but looking back towards the *Bellatrix*, and the lock gates leading to the open sea, I made up my mind: I would be going back out there.

41

3

THE TEMPTATIONS

APRIL–MAY 1987

I stayed on land just long enough to make sure that Caroline was where I wanted to be, and to tie up the loose ends I had left behind in February.

Surbiton was lovely, but it no longer felt like home; my heart was out as sea. I tuned into Caroline whenever I was at the flat, and it seemed strange to hear the music and voices coming out of the radio, and to realise that they were from that little community I had been part of, and that I could listen to my friends but not reach them. Other things seemed odd too. The ground was always solid under my feet, you could turn on the tap for as long as you liked, and you could stack things in a cupboard without worrying if they would fall over the next time the wind got up.

I wanted to rejoin the ship, but of course it wasn't that simple: I couldn't just get on a bus or a train to go there, I would have to wait to be invited. Luckily, I didn't have to wait too long: Peter Phillips and Ronan apparently liked me. I even got paid – a couple of hundred pounds – which went towards keeping my room paid for.

Towards the end of April, I got a call one evening from Cosmic saying that the *Bellatrix* would be going soon, if I wanted to go with it. I told him yes, and was pleasantly surprised to hear him sounding pleased by my answer.

On this occasion, things were better organised, and I had a little more time to prepare for the tender – a whole twenty-four hours. This time it was Tom Anderson who was doing the driving; Cosmic was apparently tied up with something else. He turned up at my place at about 1 AM on a Saturday morning, in a rather nice Mercedes which showed signs of having been driven and maintained a lot more carefully than Cosmic's Volvo. With him was a chap called John Tyler, a Caroline DJ from 1986 who had felt the call of the sea again, and a new recruit to the station, a New Zealand woman, Lucy, who was on a round-the-world tour and had talked her way on to Caroline on the basis of some shows she had done on a land-based pirate station.

We drove through the night to Dover, where we were in plenty of time for the ferry, which Tom had booked in advance. Again, there was a period of stomach-churning anxiety as we drove along the section of roadway inside Dover Eastern Docks that leads to Customs and the ferry, but, like the last time, we were not even stopped. On the other side of the Channel, Tom took the back roads to Dunkirk, as we were well ahead of schedule. I drank in the sights and sounds of the countryside, knowing that I wouldn't experience them again for a while.

As we drove, we had Caroline playing on the car radio, and Tom talked disparagingly about the music format, and complained about hearing top-forty tracks by people like Madonna and Duran Duran being played. 'I can't believe we go to all the effort of putting a ship out there in the middle of the North Sea and running a radio station just to play that shit,' he said sadly.

When we talked about the ship, Lucy expressed surprise that it was anchored in one location, rather than sailing around from country to country. 'Actually, that might be an idea,' Tom grinned. 'Do that, and get rid of the top-forty shit, and you might get me back on board.'

Lucy told us that she had two months left on her visa and, after that, she would be returning home, where her fiancé, Patrick, was waiting for her. 'At least he damn well better be still waiting,' she said. 'If he's been up to any of what I've been doing in the last four months, I'm going to kill him.'

At about 4 PM, Willie arrived to unlock the *Bellatrix*, and, once he'd seen that we were on board and had been allocated cabins, Tom gave us a friendly wave, climbed into his Mercedes and drove away. I went straight to bed.

Some hours later, I was woken by the cabin door opening and the light being switched on. Willie walked in, followed by a crowd of people. 'And this is one of the cabins where the DJs sleep as they go to and from the *Ross Revenge*,' he said, obviously giving a guided tour to whoever it was. 'This is one of the English DJs. Hello, Steve.'

'Uh . . . eh. Hi!' I said, smiling sheepishly at the crowd of gaping faces, and doing my best to cover my nudity. The faces nodded seriously at me, then filed out, turning off the light as they did so. Still very tired from the overnight ferry crossing, I went straight back to sleep again.

I awoke to find the light on again and a tall, white-haired man shaking me vigorously. Before he even spoke, I recognised him as Ronan O'Rahilly, who was so paranoid about official surveillance that he had not been out to the *Ross Revenge* since before it replaced the *Mi Amigo* four years ago. What on earth was he doing on the *Bellatrix*?

'Hey, are you Steve Conway?' he asked me, in a sort of Irish-American drawl.

'Yes,' I replied, sitting up – and banging my head on the bunk above.

'Hey, Stevie baby. Don't wake up – I'll talk to you in the morning.' And with that, he turned off the light and left.

My mind was racing, and I decided to get up. There was no way I could go back to sleep while I was wondering why Ronan was on the tender, what he wanted to speak to me about, and who the people I had seen earlier were. And besides, what sort of person wakes you up in the middle of the night to tell you to stay asleep?

I arrived upstairs to find a huge crowd of people in the *Bellatrix*'s messroom. We were already out at sea, and we would soon be arriving at the *Ross*. The large group of strangers I had seen Willie escorting round the ship were Dutch and French radio enthusiasts, who were paying Willie about thirty Dutch guilders a head for a return trip on the tender and a couple of hours of sightseeing on the *Ross*. Willie had decided that if these people were paying boatmen fifteen Dutch guilders each to travel out on cramped, uncomfortable fishing vessels and photograph the ship, they would certainly pay more to travel in style on the *Bellatrix*, where they would even meet some of the Caroline and Monique staff. He was right: they were clearly having the time of their lives.

I could only imagine the impact that the arrival of this mega-tender full of Caroline management and sightseers in the early hours of the morning would create out at the *Ross Revenge*. Boy, were they in for a surprise!

When we arrived at the Knock Deep, Ronan took charge. 'Hey, listen everyone. Hide in the shadows out on deck where no one can see you, and then give the guys a shock when we're up close.'

He got Willie to turn a very bright spotlight on to the front deck of the *Bellatrix* so that, as we came up to the *Ross*, everybody standing in the shadows on the *Bellatrix* would be invisible. The *Bellatrix* gave a blast on its horn and hovered around the *Ross*'s stern, waiting for some action. A sleepy-looking Chicago appeared on the back deck and threw a rope across, to tie the two vessels together. Kevin Turner appeared on the deck as well. Then, Ronan stepped forward into the spotlight, appearing before Kevin and Chicago's eyes as suddenly as if he'd been beamed down from the *Enterprise*. 'Hey, howya doin'?' he called across. For once, Chicago and Kevin were speechless.

More people were clambering up onto the *Ross*'s back deck now, and excited shouting could be heard, as those who saw that Caroline's owner was on the tender rushed down to get their colleagues out of bed. I was the first across to the *Ross* – and was instantly knocked down and licked all over by a very excited Raffles. Ronan and Freddie came on board soon after, and, accompanied by Kevin Turner, Peter Phillips, and Chicago, proceeded to make a grand tour of the ship. Then the visitors came over, and the *Ross* was full of excited people with cameras peering into every corner, photographing everything that moved – and a lot of things that didn't. I gave Lucy a brief tour of the ship and then excused myself, as Willie needed help bringing the supplies across from the *Bellatrix*.

As dawn broke, Ronan commandeered the newsroom for an important meeting, which Chicago, Kevin and Peter Phillips attended. As the newsreader, I ended up sitting in on it, and was able to listen in to what was going to be a historic debate about the future location of the *Ross Revenge*.

Caroline ships had used the Knock Deep as an anchorage for more than thirteen years. Now, however, legislation was being brought through Parliament which would considerably extend British jurisdiction; when the bill was passed, the Knock Deep would be inside UK waters. It would soon be time for Caroline to move.

Charts of the North Sea and Thames estuary were pored over, and a line was drawn to mark the new limit of British waters. The new anchorage would have to be much further out to sea, and much more exposed. Two locations were looked at. One of them, the Galloper, was secluded but was also much more further from the Kent and Essex coasts – and from Dunkirk. The other, the Falls Head, was close to shipping lanes but had a good path over water for our radio signal to get into London, and was just eighteen miles from Ramsgate. Ronan eventually announced that we would anchor at the Falls Head. We would stay where we were until the new act was about to become law, and we were not to tell anyone outside the room where we were going until the time came.

The meeting over, Ronan went on another tour of his ship, and then people started to make the journey back across to the *Bellatrix*, the visiting radio fans going first. Peter Phillips was also going off on this tender, so I would be working under Kevin Turner again.

Finally, everyone who wanted to had changed ships, and the *Bellatrix* did one complete circuit of us before sailing away with the customary blast on its horn, to much waving by everyone on both vessels. Normality finally settled over the *Ross Revenge* again, and I found myself a vacant cabin and moved my stuff in.

This time I settled into my newsreading straight away and felt more confident in my abilities. There was a full crew, including six DJs, so I didn't need to do any programmes, as the station was on twenty-four hours every day, with someone there specially for the 1 to 5 AM shift.

We had a cook on board as well – a chap named Derek, who harboured ambitions to be a DJ but whose demo tape had not been up to scratch. Unfortunately, his cooking wasn't all that hot either, and the situation was made worse by the knowledge that Kevin was on board and could have cooked some really tasty meals.

Derek, although a nice person to have on board, and reasonably hard-working, gave us many unintentional laughs as he performed his duties on board the vessel. On one occasion, Chicago asked him to wash and clean the main corridor of the ship, and Derek set to work with a mop and bucket, enthusiastically sloshing water around everywhere. Halfway down the corridor, he came to an electric socket, and decided that that should be thoroughly washed too . . .

There was a loud bang, an orange ball of flame appeared, and Derek went flying through the air, ending up on his back several feet down the corridor. 'What happened?' he asked in bewilderment, as we helped him to his feet.

On another occasion, Derek did something so insanely silly that it would have got him a major balling-out from Chicago, but for the fact that he simply didn't realise what he was doing. We kept a large water container in the shower room near the studios. We were restricted to one shower every four days, and instead of wasting the cold water which came out before the shower ran hot, we would save it in this container for other purposes, such as washing clothes. Fresh water was not scarce, but we still had to be careful because, if we exhausted the reserves before the next supply run, life would become very uncomfortable. One day, I was coming up the stairs to studio level when, through an open door, I caught sight of Derek pouring the entire container – two weeks' worth of saved water – down the drain. Before I could reach him, every last drop of it was gone.

'What the hell do you think you're doing?' I shouted at him, not believing what I'd just seen.

'Ah well, I'm about do some clothes washing, and I needed a big container to put some seawater in to wash with.'

'But couldn't you have used the water that was in the container?' I demanded. 'That's what we collected it for.'

'Well, I thought about that,' he replied. 'Then I decided that using fresh water for washing would be a waste, so I decided to use seawater instead.'

'So you poured two weeks' worth of saved fresh water down the drain to avoid wasting it?' I asked him.

'Er, yes,' he replied. 'Oh . . . .'

Luckily for him, we still had a reasonable amount of fresh water in the tanks at that stage and were getting regular tenders, so the wastage was not too critical.

Kevin gave Derek one day a week off, and cooked for us himself on that day – to the relief of the crew. The rest of the week, Kevin gave Derek a hard time. Kevin, although a brilliant DJ and a great cook, could be a difficult boss. If he liked you, life was reasonably easy, but if he didn't, he made sure that everyone knew it, and he was not averse to tearing strips off you in public.

Kevin's approach to running the radio station was to strive for perfection in himself and to expect it in others too. Off-air, he often let his hair down, and he had a good sense of humour, but he would not tolerate anything that got in the way of the running of the radio station, or people whom he felt were not putting in the same level of effort as he was. The station always sounded very good when he was the onboard controller, but the environment could be fraught.

Lucy, a party animal, sometimes stayed up well into the early hours of the morning, drinking beer and watching videos with the people on the later shifts, and then struggled to get up for her own 9 AM show, a little the worse for wear after too little sleep. After a week or so on late nights, when it became apparent that she was a natural broadcaster, with a good voice and a nice easy style, she had been moved to the morning slot. However, Kevin felt that she was not making any effort to stay fresh for the morning show, and the atmosphere between them soon became frosty. Inevitably, this spilled over into general life on board: we all lived together as well as working alongside each other, so workplace tensions tended to intensify on board and affect everyone. Lucy was popular with all of us, but at the same time we could understand Kevin's point.

There were added complications for me too. I liked Lucy and had become very friendly with her. I could never work out if she was aware that I found her attractive, but she would spend a lot of time talking to me about her sex life on land: she had apparently had a string of encounters while working her way around Europe. She was getting attention from some of the guys on the ship, but she told me that she wouldn't sleep with them because they just wanted her for her body, and she had no real connection with them. At the same time, she would often throw comments into the conversation with me about how sexually frustrated she was, and that she was just aching for 'a shag', as she put it. For me, still relatively inexperienced with women, and with a crush on her, being in her company was an enjoyable but at times demanding experience. I decided that it would be a bad idea to try to develop anything beyond a friendship with her, as, in the circumstances, neither of us would be able to back away if things became uncomfortable.

There were times, however, when I was tempted to the limit. One of those occasions occurred in the unlikely setting of my early-morning news duties. The news shift during Kevin Turner's breakfast show was very tightly timed: the news, weather and travel had to be spot on, of course, but there was also a schedule posted on the newsroom wall by Kevin, showing the times at which he wanted tea delivered to the studio – and woe betide me if I was late. The tea schedule was basically three times an hour, slotted around the more legitimate tasks of the newsreader, such as headlines, main news, and international news on Monique. Into this I also had to add a wake-up call and cup of coffee for the next presenter on after Kevin: Lucy. I worked it out so that I had the eight o'clock news compiled and ready by ten to the hour, then I would dash downstairs, make the coffee and bring it into her cabin, turning on her light, and shaking her if necessary. This would leave me just enough time to get back upstairs and catch my breath before the news itself.

This particular morning, I was running through the routine as usual: make Kevin's tea, compile news, read news, make Kevin's tea, compile news . . . . At 7.50, I shot down to the galley and put the kettle on, a freshly written script finished and ready upstairs. While the kettle was boiling, I got the cups ready for Lucy's coffee, Kevin's tea, and one for myself, and then walked carefully down the steep stairs to the cabins, cup in hand.

I knocked softly on Lucy's door and, getting no response, entered the room, turning on the light as I did so. I never got a reply to my knocks on her cabin, as she was a deep sleeper, but I always knocked, just in case. She was fast asleep in her bunk, with a little bundle of blonde hair peeping out from under the bedclothes. I called her gently, but she didn't stir, so I shook her through the blankets, and she still didn't move – which was unusual. I kept on trying.

'Lucy, it's time to wake up. There's a cup of coffee here for you. It's time to wake up, Lucy . . .'

Suddenly, she sat bolt upright in the bunk, the blanket falling away to reveal bare breasts. 'I think T'Pau should be on the "C" list,' she said, then buried herself under the blankets again.

I was stunned. I shook her again, but she only pulled the blankets tighter around herself, and didn't seem to hear what I was saying. I got the feeling that she was going to need more than a cup of coffee to wake her up this time. It was two minutes to eight. I would have to go, and get back down after the news to wake her. I rushed upstairs, and was just in time for the news. I stumbled through it out of breath: I kept seeing her two lovely breasts where my script should have been. It took a real effort to hold it together. Afterwards, I escaped downstairs to make Kevin yet another cup of tea, and to try to wake Lucy again.

She didn't seem to have moved since the last time I was there, and I slipped my hand under the blanket, determined to give her a good hard shake on the shoulder to snap her out of her comatose state. When my hand touched her, she grabbed it, moved it down to a warm breast and, with a sleepy moan, turned over to lie on her front, trapping my fingers in her cleavage. My head was reeling; I didn't know what to do. If I pulled my hand out, she might wake up suddenly and think I was molesting her in her sleep, but I couldn't just leave my hand there . . .

I managed gently to slide my hand out from under her, though it took a while, as every time I tried to move she would moan softly in her sleep and put my hand back to where it had been before. I tried desperately not to enjoy the feeling of her breast in my hand, but I wasn't wholly successful, and my warm feelings towards her complicated things even further. Finally I got free, and fled upstairs, shaking. I read the next news in a blur, knowing that I'd have to get her awake somehow before 9 AM, or Kevin would go absolutely bananas and would tear her to pieces. Her oversleeping and missing her programme would be just the ammunition he needed to use against her.

I approached her cabin again at 8.45 with trembling hands, a wet flannel – and confused feelings. I dabbed the wet, cold cloth on her back, and she reacted, though not in the way I'd expected. She turned over, pulled the blanket down and threw it over the side of the bunk, exposing her whole naked body to me, and lay on her back, still fast asleep, but smiling sweetly. 'Look what I've got,' she mumbled.

Poor little Catholic boy that I was, I was caught between feelings of guilt, confusion and fear. I tried to cover her with another blanket. She threw that off, and kept on pushing away anything I put near her. Still asleep, her struggles were exposing more and more of her curves and contours to me and, although I tried to avert my gaze, I couldn't keep looking away. She grabbed my hand again, ran it over her body from the breast down, all the way down . . . I gritted my teeth and, somehow, kept control of myself, though looking down at her beauty, and feeling my hand being guided over her flesh made me feel as if I was falling into a deep hole . . . falling from a great height, and all I could see was her.

Suddenly, she was pulling not just my hand, but my arm, trying to pull me into that cosy bunk and on top of her. She was mumbling in her sleep again. I pulled back, and kept pulling, deciding that if she could pull me into the bed, then I could pull her out of it. As we struggled, her mumbled words became more distinct, and she said something which made me very glad I hadn't let her win: 'Patrick . . . come on, Patrick . . . come and love me.' So that was it. In her sleep, she had felt me trying to wake her, and had imagined that I was her fiancé.

Eventually I got her out of the bunk, managing to avoid letting her fall to the floor, and sat her on a little bench. Incredibly, she was still not awake, though she seemed to be aware of her surroundings. I found some panties on the floor, and pulled them up over her unresisting legs.

'Spoilsport,' she mumbled.

'I don't know what you were on last night,' I replied, 'but when you wake up and remember what happened in here this morning, you're not going to want to see me for a month.'

'Now listen to me. I'm going to have to go upstairs to read the nine o'clock news, and then I'm going to come down here and get you up to the studio. When I come back down in a few minutes, I want to see you sitting up and getting dressed, not back in your bunk asleep – and if you are asleep, you'll get a bucket of water over you. Is that clear?'

'Mmmmmph,' said Lucy, and fell over.

I shook my head and left, calling in to the studio to see Kevin before going up to the newsroom. 'Listen, Lucy's not very well this morning,' I told him. 'But she'll be able to do her programme – she'll just be a few minutes late.'

'Has she been drinking?' he asked. 'Because if she cares so little about her programme that she's prepared to turn up hungover, then she's off as far as I'm concerned. She can do night-times until the next tender, and then she'll be off, and she won't be back.'

'No,' I replied, 'she's not hungover, she's just been sick – I think she ate something last night that wasn't properly defrosted or something.'

Kevin sighed, and said that he'd stand in for her for fifteen minutes or so, but that if she didn't come up by then, he'd have to get someone else out of bed to do her programme. As I read the nine o'clock news, my mind was still racing. Apart from anything else, there was my own state of extreme sexual frustration: I had seen a girl for whom I had feelings naked and beautiful before me, enticing me into bed, and then calling out another man's name.

'For Caroline 558, this is Steve Conway.' I read my outcue as the news ended. *I bet they don't get up to this sort of thing on Radio 4*, I thought as I left the newsroom and went back downstairs to do battle once more with our naked midmorning presenter.

I steeled myself, then knocked and entered Lucy's cabin. She was curled up on the floor, fast asleep in a corner, bless her. I lifted her up and looked into her eyes. She peered back at me with a puzzled expression on her face, and felt around her body to see if she had any clothes on.

'What . . . eh . . . where am I?' she said. She looked as if she was going to fall over again.

'In your cabin, halfway through your programme, and in deep shit unless you get up to the studio within five minutes,' I told her, though it was hard to see how much of it she was taking in.

She fumbled around a bit, but I had to do most of the dressing of her, and then she tried to get back into bed again.

'No!' I told her, grabbing her by the arm, and bundling her out the door and up the stairs. I half-carried her up to the studio, and prepared to deal with Kevin.

'It's OK now, Kevin,' I said. 'I know she looks a bit out of it, but she's just thrown up. She'll be fine to do her programme. I'll stay here for a while and make sure she's OK.'

If Kevin had chosen to stay in the studio even another minute to investigate, he would have seen that she was totally zonked, and all hell would have broken loose. But luckily, he was dying to go to the toilet (all that tea, I suppose), so he left me with her.

It was a very strange programme, but we hid it from the listeners quite well. For the first two hours, I had to operate the studio myself, as Lucy was just not capable of doing so. I sat her on the chair with wheels and kept her in a corner of the studio. I would play a few records, then wheel her across to the microphone and, when I started the next record, I would jab her in the back and say 'Speak', and turn the mike on. Then she would manage to say a few words – usually something like 'Caroline 558' and the song title. Then I would switch the mike off, wheel her back into the corner, and carry on.

Strange – but it worked. Kevin was busy elsewhere and didn't notice anything, and the listeners got plenty of back-to-back music.

About halfway through the programme, Lucy came out of her comatose state and started to take an interest in her surroundings. She was
a little puzzled as to how she was on air, with no memory of how she
had got dressed, got to the studio, or started the programme, but there
she was, and she had to accept it. By midday, she was doing everything
herself, and was quite awake, if a little subdued.

After a while, she suddenly frowned, looked at me and put her
hand up to her face. I could see the light of memory in her eyes. She
looked at me, and just raised her eyebrows.

'This morning, Steve . . . did I . . . ?'

'Yes,' I replied.

She went deep, deep red, and was silent for a while. Then she
looked at me again. 'Ah well, it's not as if it's anything you haven't seen
before, I suppose. If you've seen one, you've seen them all, I say.'

I stayed silent, thinking how little she knew of just how affected I
had been by it all.

After that, Lucy did knock some of the late-night sessions in the
mess room on the head, and started to concentrate more on being
rested and fresh for her show. This helped smooth relations with Kevin
a little until she left to return home a few weeks later.

Meanwhile, over at our neighbours on the *MV Communicator*, things
were not going well. Laser Radio had been going through some very
hard times. Their transmission masts had collapsed in a storm, and
they had not been on the air for many weeks; the ship was being staffed
by a skeleton crew of just three. Their finances were now so poor that
supporting even the three of them was difficult, and the *Communicator*
was low on almost every basic supply, including food and water. According to the crew, the whole Laser organisation was on the point of
collapse, and even Freddie and Willie hadn't been paid for the *Bellatrix*'s
tender runs to them since at least January. If it wasn't for the fact that
the *Bellatrix* had to come out to service the *Ross Revenge* anyway, Freddie would long ago have stopped supplying them with even fresh water.

Just how much trouble they were in became apparent one weekend in May, when Freddie Bolland, unable to wait any longer for the

mounting debts to be repaid, put a crew of his own on board the *Communicator*, effectively taking control of the ship. This was a source of great anxiety to the English on board the *Ross Revenge*, especially as the takeover of the *Communicator* had taken place in the dead of the night, with the *Bellatrix* arriving in the Knock Deep covertly, without lights.

We kept a constant watch on the situation from the bridge and debated what we should do if the *Bellatrix* attempted to visit us. It was decided that, as it may have committed an act of aggression against a ship in international waters, the *Bellatrix* would not be allowed to come near us until we had heard otherwise from our office, and that any attempt by it to do so would be resisted with force.

After a couple of days, we received a message from our office via a CB contact on land. He said that Ronan and Cosmic were aware of the situation and that, although they were very unhappy about it, there was nothing they could do. He then added that nobody on the *Communicator* had been harmed and that we should not be surprised by what was going to happen within the next hour. We tensely awaited the next development. Sure enough, before the hour was up we saw the *Bellatrix* pull away from the *Communicator*; we could just make out a thick metal chain between the two vessels. Slowly but surely, our one-time rival but later friend and neighbour in the Knock Deep was dragged away, until it became a little red dot on the horizon and then disappeared altogether.

The Caroline team gathered on the bridge and mourned the now-departed *Communicator*, staring up the Knock Deep to where the ship's lights usually made a bright spot in the darkness, and where now there was nothing but black. How the mighty had fallen; we were doing fine now, but one day that could be us, boarded and towed away, silenced forever.

The next week was difficult because, although we now knew what had happened to the *Communicator*, we were still wondering what Freddie had planned. Our suspicions deepened midweek, when we got a message from Chicago on land via a special personal radio link which he had installed between the ship and his house, and which he used only in emergencies. Chicago told us that Freddie had kept the

Communicator at sea, only in a different location – off the French coast near Dunkirk. The *Bellatrix* had apparently been making numerous visits to it, and Freddie possibly intended to use it rather than sell it. It was possible that Freddie would try to refurbish it, then break his contract with us, move Monique on to the *Communicator*, and leave us without a regular supplier. This way, he would have his own ship and station, which would be closer to France and Holland, and over which he would have complete control. Chicago also warned us that when Freddie next brought a tender to us, he might try to remove not only his crew but also equipment from the *Ross Revenge*, to put on the other ship. This was to be resisted absolutely, Chicago stated, because all equipment used by the Dutch on the *Ross* was owned by Caroline and was not to be removed under any circumstances.

Ronan had ordered that if Freddie did try to swap ships, we were to keep the Monique programmes going out on 963 Khz, with continuous music played by the English crew, and run all the regular Dutch adverts. We could then find another Dutch group to take the frequency over as a going concern, and make a deal for supplies from them; Freddie would have to start from scratch on a different frequency, and entice listeners, instead of having them handed to him on a plate. The possibility was also raised that the current Dutch crew on the *Ross* – who were, of course, Freddie's employees – might be aware of his plans and might have been asked to sabotage our ship or transmitters on a pre-arranged date, to clear the 963 Khz frequency for the *Communicator* and ensure that Freddie's new station took over seamlessly from the Dutch one on the *Ross*. Ronan was especially worried about this, as similar incidents had happened on pirate ships back in the 1970s, causing considerable damage and putting the stations off the air for extended periods. We were warned to be extremely careful, and to remain watchful at all times.

The movements of the Monique team on board the *Ross* were restricted: they were only allowed in their cabins, their studio, the record library, and the mess room. Our transmitter room and generator room were locked up, as was the entrance to the bridge, with access being granted to English crew members only, by whoever was on watch – an unprecedented step. The atmosphere in our normally happy little community deteriorated rapidly with the introduction of this 'ethnic segregation'.

Our next tender was due in a few days' time, and Chicago warned us not even to let the *Bellatrix* alongside us unless we could see him on board it. Ronan was flying to Holland to hold a meeting with Freddie on the Friday, in an attempt to sort out the situation: if the tender showed up with Chicago on it, everything was OK, but if he was not, then it was to be treated as unauthorised.

When Saturday came, it was extremely tense on board the ship; everywhere, little groups of two or three huddled together, discussing the situation. English and Dutch eyed each other suspiciously, and barely talked to each other. Only the programmes carried on as normal, the listeners to Caroline 558 and Monique 963 having no idea that behind the normal diet of music, news and chat, a tense drama was being played out.

On Saturday afternoon, all Caroline staff had a meeting to discuss the defence of the ship. We agreed that since the *Bellatrix* usually showed up at about 3 AM on a Sunday morning, we would all be up and ready at that time. The people who normally worked overnight would wake the rest of us at midnight, quietly, and without disturbing the Dutch, whose cabins were at the other end of the accommodation corridor. We would keep a watch in all directions and would all be armed in one way or another. When the *Bellatrix* was spotted, the tender bell would *not* be rung, and two people would guard the top of the stairs from the cabins, preventing any Dutch who might awaken from leaving their rooms.

It was difficult to get to sleep that evening, knowing what lay ahead, but I managed it and at midnight exactly was gently woken by Kevin. I dressed quietly and stole upstairs, one of a few English staff creeping away from their cabins at that moment. Kevin gave us all tea, and then it was off up to the bridge to be issued with our weapons. Mike had the ship's rifle, Kevin some distress flares, which would be quite nasty if fired directly at a ship, and I had a heavy iron bar with a wicked curved spike at the end. Various other crew members were carrying other equally deadly-looking implements; all of us were willing to defend our floating island to the last. Up on the roof of the bridge (or the 'monkey island', as it was known), Mike had rigged up an enormous ship's searchlight, which rotated. The light could be controlled from below; it cast a bright beam over the sea in any direction, like one of the searchlights used to spot planes in World War II. Various other fixed high-power spotlights (which were not generally used) were poised to be switched on when the *Bellatrix* came near. A final check downstairs showed the guards on the Dutch cabins to be *in situ* and alert, and we all dispersed to our prearranged posts; mine crouched in a corner of the monkey island.

Time passed slowly, and it seemed like forever before Mike came around on patrol to tell me that it was nearly 3 AM, and time to be extra vigilant. We scanned the horizon together: from here, the highest point on the ship, we would see the lights of the *Bellatrix* before anyone else. Always assuming they had their lights on, of course . . . About twenty minutes later, I spotted some faint lights on the horizon and called down softly to warn the others. Everybody crouched down in their positions, tension oozing from every pore. The lights gradually resolved into a set of red, green and white lights: whatever it was, it was heading straight for us. As it came closer, we could make out the familiar shape of the *Bellatrix*, and our big searchlight sprung into action, pinning the tender down in a pool of bright light, and probably dazzling Willie into the bargain. All around the *Ross*, floodlights snapped on, illuminating the crew members, who were standing along each rail and corner, on every accessible deck, each person with his or her weapon.

The *Bellatrix* hesitated, obviously unsure of what to make of this reception. Willie was used to arriving at this time of night to find the ship almost dead, rather than brightly lit, bristling with hostile faces and armed to the teeth. We kept the *Bellatrix* in the glare of the spotlight as it wallowed in the water about twenty yards away, and we waited for its next move. Suddenly, a door on the side of the tender swung open and Chicago emerged, blinking, into the light, followed by another friendly face, that of Peter Phillips. Almost as one, we breathed a big sigh of relief, put down our weapons and adopted a more welcoming posture. The *Bellatrix* slowly moved in to tie up at our stern, Willie still a little unsure about *our* intentions.

We welcomed Chicago, Peter and some fresh crew members on board, and the tension of the last week rapidly dissipated as they told us that Ronan had held very frank discussions with Freddie, threatening him with various forms of dire retribution if he broke his contract to rent our second frequency and keep us supplied, let alone take anything off the ship. The danger was past, though Chicago added that, as Freddie still had control of the *Communicator*, we could not be too careful, and tonight's show of force was probably useful in showing him that the *Ross Revenge* would not be the pushover that the Laser ship had been. After a short while the *Bellatrix* departed, taking with it Kevin Turner and Mike Watts and leaving us with the more relaxed management team of Chicago and Phillips.

A change of Dutch crew had also helped calm things down a little, as the old one had, quite understandably, been getting more than a little angry at our increasingly draconian treatment of them.

Things were looking up.

4

THE MOVE

The beginning of summer 1987 saw Radio Caroline running smoothly once more. Relations with our Dutch colleagues on Monique had returned to their usual state of friendly rivalry. It wasn't long before we had new matters to occupy us, as political developments took place in the UK which directly affected the ship.

Margaret Thatcher had called a general election for June. Apart from giving me more to do in the newsroom, this resulted in the Territorial Sea Bill (the new law extending British jurisdiction to cover the Knock Deep) coming into effect more quickly than expected. This was one of a number of Bills that were rushed through the House with Opposition consent before Parliament broke up.

As a result, plans to move the ship were brought forward, and in the end they were put into effect on 10 June, the day before the general election. As the *Ross* did not normally move under its own steam, Ronan arranged for a large tug to visit us and assist in the move, particularly with the raising and checking of the thousand-foot-long anchor chain. In order to protect the tug's crew from possible legal action, we would not be broadcasting while they were alongside us.

The day of the move, everyone on board was awake and about early. Peter Phillips and I went through the breakfast show as normal, advising listeners that we would be closing down at 8 AM sharp 'in order to carry out essential work on the *Ross Revenge*'. Generally,

Caroline was rarely off the air for long, but we did spend one or two full days a year off-air to carry out major mast work. We had an extra engineer, Keith, on board to look after our big old Werkspoor engine, which was purring away like a pussy cat, sending shivers and throbs the length and breadth of the ship.

Just before 8 AM, I read the news over a background noise of throbbing engines and excited voices. At the end of the bulletin, Peter announced: 'The time is now two minutes to eight o'clock, and Radio Caroline is closing down in order to carry out some essential work. We anticipate being back on the air in about six hours' time, although the work may take a little longer. In any case, we will return to the airwaves as soon as is technically possible. On behalf of the captain and crew of the radio ship *Ross Revenge*, I'd like to wish you a very good day, and hope that you'll rejoin us later.' The station theme, 'Caroline', by the Fortunes, then played out, finishing at exactly 8 AM. A few seconds later, the two 'Transmitter Fail' lights in the 558 studio lit up brightly, indicating that 558 and 963 were now off the air and it was safe for the tug, the *Onrust*, to move in.

The tug's crew attached cables and chains to our anchor chain and began the long task of hauling it up. By 11 AM, the big black anchor, weighing several tons, lay dripping on the deck. Then, with little cere-mony, the *Onrust* and the *Ross* turned their engines up to full-ahead and, with the tug firmly lashed alongside us and doing the steering, the two ships swung round and sailed down and out of the Knock Deep like a pair of nautical Siamese twins. Within minutes, Caroline's home of many years had been left behind us and we were off for pastures new.

In order to follow the shipping lanes, we had to sail in towards the Kent coast and then parallel to it, rather than cutting across on a more direct route. This meant that for several hours we were well inside British waters, and indeed only a few miles off the coast. For a large part of the journey, we must have been easily visible from the shore: we could see the land and the seaside towns as we headed on our way.

By mid-afternoon, we had passed Margate, and now Kent was falling behind us as we headed out towards the open sea again. At about 3 PM, we spotted a small blue blob on the horizon. Looking at it through the binoculars, it turned out to be the *Bellatrix*, seemingly on an unscheduled supply run. Presumably even Willie had not been told we were moving: he looked to be heading towards the Knock Deep! Eventually, he spotted us and swung round behind us, following us to wherever we were going. A passenger ferry passed close by in the other direction, its passengers waving and smiling at us from its decks.

We soon passed the limit of what would be the new British Territorial Waters, and at 5 PM precisely our anchor was dropped with a massive splash into the deep blue waters of the Falls Head. A small black-and-yellow flashing buoy made a convenient landmark a quarter of a mile away, and we could just see the Isle of Thanet in the far distance. We were now much closer to France – which would make the *Bellatrix*'s tendering runs much easier.

The Falls Head definitely had a different feel from the Knock Deep. For one thing, paradoxically, although we were further out to sea, we could now see land clearly most of the time, and there was a steady stream of shipping passing by: it was like watching traffic going by on a motorway. Some of the ships used the Falls Head buoy as a turning point to swing left or right and head up the Thames towards London. These ships came very close to us, their crews coming out to stare and wave at the *Ross Revenge* and its towering mast.

Within minutes of dropping our anchor, the tug disengaged from us and fled the scene, and by 5.30 PM Caroline 558 was back on the air. No sooner had the tug left than the *Bellatrix* started sending people across to us in the rubber speedboat. Willie had sensibly decided not to hang the extra weight of a large ship off the *Ross* while her anchor was still finding a hold on the seabed.

The following day was not only our first full day in our new location but also election day in the UK. After consulting with Peter, I ramped up the news output, doing bulletins throughout the night as the results came in. I double-headed these with Jackie Lee, so that one of us summarised the main points while the other went into detail on individual results.

Jackie, who had joined us a few weeks earlier, was a real find: she was a very talented broadcaster and easy to get on with. She had a good knowledge of music – and the sense to keep her spoken links short and intelligent (instead of babbling on like an idiot, as many DJs do). She also had a lovely voice. She started off on a late-evening programme, but Peter quickly realised her worth and moved her to the mid-morning show, directly after his breakfast programme. Jackie quickly blended into Knock Deep society, and was willing to do lots of extra work as well as her shift on air. She helped run the 'God Tapes' – the American-sponsored religious programmes that went out on Viewpoint 963 – and her cooking was a welcome improvement on some of what had gone before.

Chicago, meanwhile, was working hard to improve the studio and transmission facilities on board the ship. One such project, which had been going on for a period of months, had involved procuring new parts and making changes to the 558 transmitter in order to increase our signal quality and range. Chicago, who liked to keep such projects close to his chest until they were completed, casually announced at the dinner table one evening that he had just finished refurbishing the transmitter and that, as of today, we had more than doubled in power, from four kilowatts to eight and a half on 558. This was terrific news: it meant that our signal would now be rock solid across the UK, even at night, and our reach into Continental Europe would be boosted.

Although they were usually in the background, the onboard engineers quickly came into their own when things went wrong, and they generally got us up and running again quickly. They had to know how to fix not only the specialist transmitting gear but also all the engine-room equipment, as well as dealing with problems with the antenna system – which often involved them having to climb to dizzying heights.

Stays (guy wires) on the mast broke every now and again. With such a tall mast on a moving base (the ship), every stay was essential to ease and balance the loading pressures on the mast. There were dozens of stays, radiating out from the tower at various different heights and in all directions. The stays had small ceramic insulators at various points, to prevent them from acting as a pathway to ground for the high-voltage broadcast power. The system was finely balanced to provide maximum support for the mast in every direction. As a result, broken stays and cracked insulators had to be replaced as soon as possible. The normal procedure was for the station to close down and go off air for a couple of hours so that some experienced crew members could climb up and fix whatever problem had arisen. In addition to urgent repairs, once or twice a year we would close down for the greater part of a day and have the entire mast and support system inspected by professional riggers.

The summer weeks passed in a blur of hazy, hot days and calm, peaceful nights, and I slipped off for some shore leave for a while in July. I went to visit my brother in Ireland, with a view to getting him to come out to the ship too. Chris had worked in the radio industry for many years, as a presenter on a number of pirate stations in Dublin and on BLB (Bray Local Broadcasting) in County Wicklow. He had always been an admirer of Radio Caroline and now wanted to join me on the high seas. Chris put together a demo tape while I was staying in Dublin, and I wrote a note to Peter, detailing Chris's successful career and recommending him as a new hire for Caroline. I counselled Chris that, if the Caroline organisation ran true to form, he would probably hear nothing for weeks, then suddenly be snatched away at breakneck speed in the middle of the night.

I was back on board the *Ross* in August, in time for a very special weekend for Caroline's fans: the commemoration of the twentieth anniversary of the British government's Marine Offences Act, which had made it illegal for advertisers, suppliers and contributors to Caroline to interact with the station. There was to be a big supporters' convention on land, and we were expecting many visitors to come out on sightseeing trips.

For many years on Caroline, supporters of the station had been known as 'anoraks' – a usage of the word that long predated its more disparaging connotations. Radio fans were proud to be known as 'anoraks' and even subscribed to a newsletter called *Anoraks UK*, which gave listings and details of pirate stations on land and at sea. (Jackie felt that the term 'anorak' was not classy enough and insisted that we refer to them as 'aardvarks' instead.)

The *Bellatrix* turned up with about thirty French and Belgian 'aardvarks', and two small boats from the UK arrived with further supporters. The attitude among the crew to aardvark visitors was always very mixed, with some people turning their nose up at the fans – even though they happily accepted the gifts that they brought. For my part, I well remembered coming out to view the ship as a fan myself, and always made an effort to be as accommodating as possible, giving guided tours of the ship.

By mid-afternoon, all the visitors had departed, and we thought we were on our own again. However, while I was working upstairs preparing a script for the 5 PM news, I spotted something strange heading towards us. I alerted the others, and we watched, fascinated, as this strange object slowly drew closer. It looked like a 1950s bus shelter, or perhaps a small bicycle shed, and it was swaying from side to side in the flat, calm sea like the pendulum of a grandfather clock. Eventually, this wobbling monstrosity got close enough for us to see that it was a boat of sorts, and packed full of friendly faces. It was the *Galexy*, a former river ferry, newly purchased by John Burch's Caroline Movement, and full of our most dedicated followers

Usually the Caroline Movement people came out to us in smaller boats, but the *Galexy* had been purchased for the longer trips needed to get to the Falls Head and because they wanted to transport their members in comfort and style. We gave the *Galexy* eight out of ten for comfort, and one out of ten for style. The unusual spelling of 'Galexy' was taken by us to be a mistake, until it was pointed out to us that the skipper's name was Alex, and that, as he felt that the sun, moon and stars revolved around him, he felt it only fitting that 'Alex' should be at the centre of the *Galexy*!

Eventually the sightseers left, sailing away into the sunset.

A few days later, we had a most unexpected visitor. One misty morning, what should come sailing over the horizon towards us but the *Communicator*! We were amazed to see our former neighbours from the Knock Deep appearing at the Falls Head, and were jubilant when we learned that the ship's original owners, the Laser organisation, had paid off the ship's debts and taken back control of it.

Laser had not been on the air for four or five months, but Paul Jackson, the sole occupant of the ship, had high hopes that things would get better now that they at least had the ship back. He sailed around us a few times, talked to us on the ship-to-shore radio and then dropped anchor about half a mile away. It was just like old times.

A few hours later, we had a visit from a couple of British government investigators, pretending to be aardvarks. Their cover was easy to blow: they came out in a very fast speedboat and asked all the wrong questions. We refused to let them on board. They sailed around the two ships, shooting video footage and asking us questions about Ronan, the ship's registration and whether there was a captain on board. They also asked about the ownership of the two vessels.

The *Communicator* was to stay with us for four or five days, before slipping off into the morning mist one day in search of a calmer anchorage closer to land. (They could get away with being anchored within UK waters because they were not currently an active radio ship.)

On 1 September, we had a visit from a supply boat that was a truly significant occasion, as it not only brought us a new captain but also took away our longest-standing crew member – Raffles – who, after four years on board, was developing an allergy to the salty atmosphere and was finally going to accompany Chicago home on a tender.

On board the supply boat *Windy*, as well as the usual new Dutch and English crew was an enormously fat man called Captain Jim, who had great difficulty getting onto the *Ross* because of his size. Mike, Peter and the others simply climbed up over the side of the *Ross* as usual, but Captain Jim had to be lifted. After many failed attempts, we eventually managed to move him up to the side of the *Ross*, balance him on the railings on his stomach as if he was a sack of potatoes, swivel him round so that his feet pointed towards the *Ross*, and then push him so that he fell off the side and landed in a heap on the deck. As he swung round, he had managed to kick Chicago in the teeth – not the ideal way to start your career with Caroline.

Peter told us that Captain Jim was joining us for a while as a proper marine captain, as part of one of Ronan's periodic drives to get the ship running extra-smoothly and to make sure that it was manned by legally qualified crew in the run-up to winter. (Normally, the broadcast engineer acted as captain. With the ship permanently anchored, we had little need of a captain, although it was still a legal requirement to have one.)

The tender stayed all night and, in the morning, Kevin, Chicago and some others boarded it for the trip back to land. Then, after four years of never knowing anything but the ship, Raffles was lifted up over the side of the *Ross Revenge* by Mike, and carefully handed down into Chicago's arms on the tender. The poor dog looked scared half to death, but when he realised that Chicago would be with him on this strange new boat, he perked up a little and began to sniff around.

Captain Jim, our new marine 'expert', soon turned out to be more of a hindrance than a help. He seemed to be taking his captain's duties far too seriously – with disastrous consequences for the harmony of life on board. In his mind, the *Ross Revenge* was a ship which just happened to have a radio station on it; in our minds, the *Ross Revenge* was a radio station which just happened to be a ship. Pretty soon, the new captain was on a collision course with virtually the entire crew. The problems started the second day he was on board, when he told the assembled crew at dinner that he thought we were lacking morale and moral guidance, and that he was initiating a programme to improve mind and body. Everyone, without exception, was to report to the back deck for organised games the following afternoon at 3 PM. The radio stations were to be shut down for the duration, to allow full attendance of the crew. We all politely declined and were informed that it was compulsory. We sighed, and said nothing, knowing that neither Peter Philips nor Mike Watts would contemplate shutting the station down for such a reason.

Captain Jim's confrontation with Mike Watts was to come sooner rather than later, following his discovery that the we used the ship's chart room, situated off the bridge, as the Caroline 558 newsroom. Jim demanded that all crew, including myself, should be banned from the chart room, as it should be for qualified ships officers only. This happened in the middle of my morning news shift, and when I refused to leave the newsroom, Jim went barging straight into the engineer's cabin, situated off the newsroom, to wake Mike up and lay down the law to him. Mike, not the most easy of people to wake at the best of times, had only just gone to bed after having been up for forty-eight hours non-stop, due to some engineering problems. Harsh words and raised voices were heard from the engineer's cabin, and Jim emerged looking very pale. No more was said about the newsroom, thought Peter commiserated with me that 'we all have to put up with these lunatics that Ronan sends out from time to time.'

The next few days were very demoralising for Jim, as he watched us taking our orders from Peter and Mike and realised that no one on the ship saw him as a figure of authority. The situation became even more funny a couple of days later, when we had the first mild winds of autumn. It was only a south-westerly force 4 or 5, just enough to make the boat rock gently, and not enough to affect anyone on board – except Captain Jim, who was violently seasick for three days.

Apart from Captain Jim, things carried on much as usual. I began to get drawn into helping Peter with the station administration and the music format. My computer, which I had brought out from home in August, started to come into its own, taking a lot of the drudgery out of his day-to-day work. Many things – oldies playlists, advert running orders and memos – needed to be typed each day, and the record playlist had to be updated each time the new UK top forty was announced.

Over the years, Radio Caroline had gone through many different musical phases, from easy listening and pop in the 1960s, through progressive rock and album tracks in the early to mid-1970s to a very eclectic free-format period at times in the mid-1980s, when you might hear pop from one presenter, rock from another, and blues and reggae at various times of the night, depending on who was on. Following Caroline's move to 558 Khz in November 1985, Ronan had decided that the station should go back to its populist roots of the 1960s, when it had played the hits of the day along with breaking new material.

The format devised by Peter split the airtime exactly 50/50 between current material and back catalogue (or 'oldies'). The current material was made up of chart hits (tracks in the top forty) and new releases, giving a breakdown of 50 percent old tracks, 30 percent top forty, and 20 percent new releases.

In the studio, the presenter followed two 'format clocks' – one for odd hours, one for even hours – which dictated which category of music was to be played at any given time. For the odd hour (i.e. 9 AM, 11 AM, 1 PM, 3 PM), the presenter would start with an 'A' (currently high in the top forty) followed by a 'Z' (a recent hit which had dropped out of the charts between three and twelve months ago), then a 'C' (a new release by a lesser-known or new artist), then a 'Sixties', then a 'B' (from the bottom half of the top forty, going up), then an 'Eighties', then a 'C+' (a new release from a well-known band or one we really supported), then a 'Seventies', and so on. Other categories included 'URB' (a Motown/soul track from the 1960s or 1970s) and 'R' (a track in the top forty but falling).

The odd- and even-hours clocks had a different running order and different balances between the various categories, so that current top-forty hits and new releases were spread evenly throughout the day, with different speeds of rotation, coming round quickly (every four to five hours for 'A' or 'C+' tracks), at medium speed (every seven to ten hours for 'B' and 'C' tracks) or very slowly (about every twenty hours for 'R' tracks). The rotation of the current material was controlled by a box of little index cards in the studio, and the cards were shuffled every morning to make sure that the tracks were in a different order every day. The current tracks were changed every Sunday night, depending on the new top forty, and any new releases we had received. The oldies rotation, which made up the other half of the music format, was very broadly based compared to most commercial stations, and included tens of thousands of tracks so that an oldie, once played, would not be heard again on the station for between four and six weeks, and then at a different time of day.

As I helped Peter more and more, I became aware of the complex decisions needed to keep the station sounding good week after week, and the reasons why the current rotation lists were structured in the way they were. Of course, keeping Caroline sounding fresh as far as new music was concerned also depended on a regular supply of records and music press, which depended on regular tendering. An English tender which was meant to arrive a few days after the *Windy* never showed up, and, indeed, more than two weeks passed without another Dutch tender, so new music was getting a bit thin on the ground. (Peter had other ways of getting new music, of course, such as recording it off the Radio 1 chart show on a Sunday and putting it onto cartridge, or borrowing new records from the Dutch DJs on Monique.)

Mike and Peter decided to make a symbolic gesture to stir our land organisation into action. Chicago had brought a little fibreglass dinghy with an outboard motor to the ship during the summer, and it was stored out on the starboard deck, for use in an emergency. The two decided to use it for a shopping trip to land, during which they could phone Cosmic, Tom or whoever was around, and put a flea in their ear. Peter had a reasonable amount of money with him, so they would be able to buy some records, oil and other essentials, even if they didn't meet up with anyone on land. They waited for a calm day and planned to set off for Margate after Peter finished on air. They would spend an hour or two on shore and be back on the ship in time for dinner. Captain Jim was not too happy about being left without an engineer on board, even for a few hours, but Mike convinced him that the trip was necessary.

Peter and Mike came to see me before they departed, for what they called 'a serious chat'. They explained that they were not happy leaving the ship with Captain Jim on board, as goodness knew what he would do while they were gone. They wanted me to understand that I must closely watch the situation on board, and step in if I felt it was necessary. They wanted to make it clear to me that the ship, and more especially the radio station, would be in my hands while they were not on board, as I was the longest-serving crew member apart from them. Mike then commented that, although they planned to be back in a few hours, I had better be prepared for the one-in-a-million chance of their not returning, due to arrest or mishap.

He took me down to the engine room and gave me a lightning tour of the daily tasks necessary to keep fuel flowing to the generator room, and also showed me how to turn the transmitters on and off. Peter then gave me the key to the 'format cupboard' – a padlocked storage space in the newsroom which only the acting programme controller had access to, and which contained important station documents, ship's papers, and the music card-index. Weighed down by this responsibility, and hoping that I wouldn't have to use all the knowledge that Mike had tried to impart to me about fuel valves, day tanks and circuit breakers, I watched with a heavy heart as the two climbed down into the little craft and cast off. It was only seven months since I had come on board the *Ross Revenge* as a nervous new crew member, and now here I was, just twenty-three, alone with a crew of people all newer to it than I was, entrusted with keeping the generators going, the ship lit, and the radio station on the air and running smoothly. And I also had to cope with a lunatic captain who would probably be the first to go to pieces if anything went wrong.

I worked through the day as usual, with things running smoothly, and no problems from Jim. The final news of the day came at 6 PM, and then I went downstairs to join the rest of the crew for dinner. A few curious faces were looking at me.

'Steve, shouldn't Mike and Peter have been back by now?' asked Jackie, concern in her voice. 'You don't think anything's happened to them, do you?'

'No, I'm sure they've just stopped off for a pint before coming back. They'll probably come alongside when we're halfway through dinner and spoil our meal – you'll see.'

But there was no sign of the little speedboat by 7 PM, and it was getting dark. The crew were becoming restless, and Captain Jim was pacing up and down muttering about how they could have been drowned or arrested and might never come back. His agitation was getting through to the others. I sent Captain Jim off to get something from the food stores and, in his absence, quickly reassured the others. I told them that, regardless of anything Captain Jim might say, I was sure that the two were quite safe and would be back soon. I looked around at the crew to see how they were reacting. Jackie, Andy Robin and Paul Grahame, who had been out to the ship before and knew me well, looked reassured, but our latest recruit, DJ Simon West, looked like he was still far from happy with things.

In reality, I was far from happy with things myself. I knew that something must have happened to Mike and Peter – and also that there was little that we, stuck out on the ship, could do about it. I knew not to let my worries show, however: I guessed that pretty soon Captain Jim would be doing enough panicking for all of us. I was right about the captain: as evening turned into night and it became obvious that the two men were not coming back, he started telling anyone who would listen that we were in terrible danger and that without Mike on board the ship would sink before morning. I followed him around, reassuring anyone he had alarmed that nothing would happen to the ship.

In fact, I could cope with little other than routine tasks, but there was no point in alarming them unnecessarily. Nonetheless, although we might have a generator breakdown or a transmitter failure, the ship was certainly not going to sink. I wandered down among the throbbing machinery in the generator room and then made my way into the engine room to check on the level of fuel in the day tank, as Mike had taught me to do only hours before.

The day tank, as its name implied, held enough fuel for just over a day of full operation – although without the ship's main engine running, the fuel would actually last two or three days. Mike had pumped it full before he left, and I could see from a little gauge pipe that it was still two-thirds full now. However, it would be no harm to top it up again. The *Ross Revenge* carried hundreds of thousands of litres of diesel fuel in vast swimming-pool-sized tanks which ran under the floor of the engine room and other parts of the ship. This was topped up with 15,000 to 25,000 litres of fuel every time the *Bellatrix* visited us, but there was always at least 100,000 litres in reserve, so that the ship could withstand a long period without supplies. Some of this fuel had to be pumped up from the bowels of the ship into the day tank every day. The day tank was high up in the top of the engine room, so the fuel flowed from there to the generators by gravity.

I stood by the ship's main fuel-transfer pump in the depths of the engine room and prayed that I had remembered Mike's instructions correctly. The *Ross Revenge* had more than twenty different tanks, all of which were connected through this pump; by opening or closing valves, you could transfer fuel from one tank to another. If I didn't open the right valves, though, I could end up sending the fuel to some forgotten corner of the ship where it would be of no use, or even pumping it overboard by accident! I concentrated hard.

Right, the fuel would be coming out of Number 7 starboard tank. That must be this valve over here. I grabbed the valve rod and screwed open the outlet valve of that tank. This necessitated putting the rod through a little inspection hatch in the floor and twisting it for what seemed like hours. Then the next step: the inlet valve to the fuel pump. Now where was that?

I looked around, and then suddenly remembered that it was under the floor beneath my feet. Again, a little section of metal flooring pulled up to reveal two of the big metal valves underneath. I inserted the rod down through the hole and opened the one which had 'Pump' marked on it in chalk. (Being a former Icelandic trawler, the *Ross Revenge* had full instructions and labels on all items of equipment – in Icelandic! Luckily, someone had gone around with the chalk afterwards.) Finally, I climbed up two levels of stairs to open the inlet valve to the day tank. That must be it: tank outlet valve, pump inlet valve, tank inlet valve, all open. Now for the moment of truth.

I stood in front of the fuel-transfer pump and twisted the little round wheel that made it go. It sprung into life with a whirr, and there was a momentary dimming of lights as the generators adjusted to the increased electrical load. The sound of gushing diesel could be heard through the pipes. I dashed up to the day tank and saw, to my relief, that the level of diesel in the little gauge-pipe was rising; I went back down to the pump and waited. After a while, the fuel-overflow sight-glass beside the pump became red with flowing diesel, so I knew I had filled the day tank to the very top. The overflow of fuel would flow harmlessly through the overflow pipe into another tank, from where it could be pumped back into the main system at a later stage. I couldn't believe it – I'd done it!

Concentrating on getting the fuel pumped up to the day tank had taken my mind off our missing crew members, but now I looked at my watch and saw that it was well past 11 PM. Something bad must have happened to them. I went into the transmitter room and watched the various electrical scopes and meters dancing away, their lights flashing and their needles flickering. Dozens of different items of equipment, most of them extremely complicated and expensive, were needed to take the sound from the studio, process it and pass it to the transmitters and up the mast into the aerial. If anything went wrong with this lot, all I would be able to do would be turn the 'Off' switch.

I went back up into the main part of the ship and found that no one had gone to bed: everyone was sitting up, straining to hear the buzz of an outboard motor appearing out of the night. Captain Jim was beside himself with anxiety, not for the missing crew, but for his own skin: he was certain that we were facing disaster. He started telling us that he would haul up our anchor and sail us into Ramsgate, and surrender the ship to the British authorities, if the engineer didn't return soon. We pointed out that if he did this, several thousand enraged Caroline supporters would throttle him the second he stepped off the ship.

It was now nearly midnight, and I thought that it was time I made some decisions. One of the items in the format cupboard was a top-secret code list, with which we could communicate emergency messages to the office over the air on the radio station itself, without listeners – or the authorities – noticing. There was a list of about two hundred codes covering all eventualities; by combining a series of codes, you could send quite complicated messages. Someone from the organisation on land would always be listening out for coded messages on the station at midday and midnight. The code list was frequently updated and, to make it even more unbreakable, you added the day's date to the code number, so that it was different virtually every time it was used. We very rarely had to use our codes, but when we did they would be slipped into the programme as part of a spoken link (e.g. 'Hello to Maria, who's listening at No. 37 Victoria Road . . . '). I got the list and spread it out on the newsroom table. I eventually settled on the codes that meant 'Engineer required' and 'DJ No. 1 [the breakfast DJ] departed'. On hearing those, the office would spring into action, knowing that if we were asking for an engineer and a breakfast DJ, something must have happened to Mike and Peter.

Just as I was about to put the list away, Captain Jim burst into the newsroom, demanding that we start announcing on air that we had lost two men. I told him that we would do no such thing and that I had matters in hand; anyway, such an announcement would bring the coastguard down on us like a ton of bricks. Plus, if Mike and Peter were on the way back out to us, search-and-rescue efforts by the authorities would intercept them, and they would be locked up. I explained that, by sending a code to the office, things could be dealt with on shore, and, if the two still could not be found, they could be reported as ordinary persons missing at sea; in this way, when they were found, they wouldn't be arrested. Jim reluctantly agreed, but I could see from his attitude that he was gradually losing his grip and might break into outright panic and do something silly at any moment. To mollify him, I got out the code list again and allowed him to pick one extra code which he thought should be sent. He decided on 'Contact ship – urgent' but, unfortunately for him, he got muddled up and presented me with a completely wrong number.

My codes went out on air at midnight, along with the number he had given me – which, when decoded, translated as: 'Captain incompetent, please send replacement'! Captain Jim, having described himself so accurately, now announced that he would spend the night in the captain's chair on the bridge, in a state of constant vigilance. We found him there fifteen minutes later, snoring his head off.

Having alerted the office to our plight, I now had to decide what to do with the radio station. Without Peter, someone else would have to do the breakfast show, and the four remaining DJs would have to cover the five shifts. I reworked the schedule so that Jackie would do Peter's breakfast show but continue for an extra hour, until 10 AM, then the others would do five hours each after her, through to the usual 1 AM closedown. I would continue to read the news, take over all of Peter's administrative duties and try my best to keep the ship's systems functioning.

I stayed up through the rest of the night, as did Jackie, and we paced around on deck looking out to sea in case, by some miracle, our problems would be solved. Finally we conceded defeat, and Jackie went off to the library to pull out the records for the breakfast show. We knew that in a few minutes, when she came on air, Peter's absence would be impossible to hide. As Jackie started setting up the studio, I went down to the transmitter room to switch the 558 signal back on. To my relief, the transmitter turned on easily, all its dials and meters showing what appeared to be normal readings.

I came back out onto the deck, heading for the studio. As I walked along the side of the ship, I caught a faint but unmistakable buzzing sound coming across the water. I waited with bated breath as it came closer and closer, until suddenly our little rubber dinghy came into the little pool of light cast by the *Ross*'s lights and I saw Mike and Peter grinning broadly and waving at me.

I poked my head into the ship and gave a whoop of joy to alert the others, then went back to the side railings. I threw a rope to the pair and helped them clamber on board the *Ross*, and we hauled the boat up after them.

'Ah, Steve . . . good morning to you,' said Peter. 'I'm just in time for my day job, I think, eh?'

We whisked the two indoors and plied them with mugs of tea, refusing to allow either of them to leave the mess room until they'd told us what had happened.

It was quite simple really. They had reached Margate within two hours, as planned, but when they returned from their shopping expedition they found the tide fully out, and their dinghy stranded in the mud. They had had to wait several hours for the tide to come in again, and then their departure had been delayed by another several hours by the need to avoid the suspicious eyes of a patrolling Customs man. Finally, on the way back out to the *Ross*, the outboard motor had broken down, and they had drifted aimlessly in the dark for two hours before Mike managed to fix it.

Everyone was up by now, and we were all delighted that we had our missing men back – even more so when Peter produced out of his shopping bag two dozen Mars bars, and announced that he had bought us two each. By now it was 5 AM, and Peter had to rush up to the Caroline 558 studio to start his programme, still clad in thick waterproofs and a life jacket. Caroline sprang into life again, with Peter Phillips on the breakfast show as usual. The listeners would never know he had been missing, never guess at the tension and anxiety behind the previous day's broadcasts.

'Good morning to you, Caroline 558, Peter Phillips in with you on the breakfast programme through until nine. Here's the Pet Shop Boys.' Peter sailed through his first link of the day, then turned round, a puzzled expression on his face. 'Oh . . . we got your codes last night. The office knew about our problem already, of course, because we had phoned them earlier, and we were sitting listening to Caroline in a late-night café at the time.

'Just one thing I want to know, though,' said Peter, his puzzled frown deepening. 'Why did you have to tell us the captain was incompetent? We knew that already.'

5

The Waterboys

September–October 1987

After the night of the missing crew members, Captain Jim became very withdrawn: he knew he'd shown himself to be a useless deadweight as far as we were concerned. Luckily, the Dutch tender *Windy* arrived not long afterwards, and he was able to head quietly home, never to return to the ship again. Quite a few crew went off on the *Windy*, but we gained a new DJ in the form of my brother, who would broadcast under the name Chris Kennedy. I was thrilled to see him on the ship, and helped him settle in. Chris confessed to me that being out on the ship was, in fact, far less unsettling than another aspect of Caroline which he had encountered on shore: Cosmic's driving. Apparently he had been picked up from a railway station by Cosmic in the early hours of the morning, when he was still feeling delicate after a long overnight journey, and had been subjected to the usual ninety-miles-an-hour screeching-tyres routine, which Cosmic had described as 'a pleasant spin'.

Peter started him off on the 9 PM to 1 AM late-night show, where all newcomers go, and he soon proved his worth, presenting excellent programmes. For a lot of the week, his late nights and my early mornings meant that we didn't see much of each other, apart from at dinnertime. Over the weekend, however, I was on straight after him at 1 AM doing my overnight shows again: eight hours solid of Caroline coming from one family.

There was something very special about manning the studio through the night on Caroline, weaving a musical spell for the thousands of people across the UK who were working at night, travelling, or just lying in bed awake. You could almost feel a connection to them – a thin tendril of empathy radiating out into the night sky across Europe. With the studio lights turned down low, and the portholes open, there was just the sea, the stars and the music.

Dawn would come, showing itself first as the faintest lightening of the horizon. Gradually, the sea turned from black to dark blue, then blue, and grey and green. After finishing the show, I would stay up, savouring the sun rising over the open sea and the wonderful freshness in the air. It was beautiful beyond belief. On weekdays, too, when I had to get up for the news shift, I never minded the early start: that first gulp of fresh sea air as I went out on deck to check the wind and sea conditions was reward enough.

Then came the first of the autumn storms – and the first sign that the Falls Head was not always such a friendly place. It was a north-westerly force 8, no worse than I had experienced already in the Knock Deep, but it had a dramatic effect on the ship. No gentle rolling from side to side this time: the ship bucked and lurched under our feet, sending people and loose objects flying from one side of the room to the other. The sea outside was whipped up into a white frenzy, and we realised just how much protection we had had from those invisible sandbanks at our old anchorage.

For twelve hours the storm blew, and the ship swung from side to side abruptly, caught between the tidal currents pulling it one way and the wind and waves trying to push it another. I was on washing-up duty that evening with a Dutch DJ and eventually had to rope in Chris as extra help, so that we had one person to wash, one to dry – and one to hold the piles of crockery and make sure they didn't go smashing onto the floor before they could be put away. It was quite comical at times, the three of us struggling to stay on our feet as wave after wave buffeted the ship, the moaning of the wind and the occasional glimpse of a high white wave through the porthole providing a surreal counterpoint to the voice of a preacher issuing from a speaker in the galley. (Chris was also on Viewpoint-tape duty and had to keep an ear cocked for when the religious tapes needed to be changed.) Suddenly the Falls Head seemed a bleak and inhospitable place.

Finishing the washing up, I said goodnight to my colleagues and made my way down the steep stairs to the cabin corridor. Down here, you couldn't hear the wind, but the motion of the ship was stronger, as you were below the centre of gravity, and I had to hold on tight to avoid losing my balance. As I went into my cabin, there was a huge wave and a particularly violent lurch. I grabbed the door frame to steady myself, just as the door slammed shut with great speed. The tips of my fingers were caught in the door, and I went down on the floor in excruciating pain. After a few minutes, it was apparent that nothing was broken, though my fingers were almost twice their normal size, and throbbing like hell. For months afterwards, I had a series of black lines across my fingernails – a constant reminder for the rest of that winter to be careful in storms.

That night, the ship rolled heavily for hours, and it was hard to relax enough to fall asleep while at the same time bracing myself to prevent rolling out of the bunk. Now I could see why the bunks had high sides and a coffin-like shape. I burrowed deep under the covers, hearing the waves crashing against the hull, and eventually fell asleep.

In October, an English tender took a number of people away without bringing out any replacements, though it did at least supply us with a brand new teletext TV for the newsroom. After this, the remaining presenters all worked extra hours to cover for the shortfall of DJs, and I volunteered to run half of the religious broadcasts on 963 and take over cooking for the whole crew as well, as Jackie had gone ashore. The cooking was no problem: it was basically the same as cooking a normal meal, except that you did twelve times as much of everything.

Working on the 'God tapes' was quite fun really. I had always stayed clear of the Viewpoint operation, because, as newsreader, my 5 AM start meant that I had to get to bed early in the evening. Now, however, we were so short-staffed that I agreed to stay up until 9 PM each night to run the first half of the tapes.

Weekends were now extremely tiring for me, with a full news day, cooking, Viewpoint, and then a four-hour programme. But I enjoyed it nonetheless. All the crew on board were happy and, as often seemed to happen, it was more enjoyable with a few people working harder, than with a large crew on normal shifts

We were promised another supply boat for the following Friday, to resolve our staffing issues, but as the weather gradually got worse, we began to realise that relief was out of the question. It was 15 October 1987 – the day before the 'Great Hurricane' hit.

The next morning started as normal for me, with a banging on my cabin door from Peter. Unknown to any of us at this stage, the whole of south-east England was being devastated by hurricane-force winds, which were causing immense destruction to property, as well as injury and loss of life. Thousands of trees were being uprooted, roofs were being torn off, and electricity cables and TV transmitter masts were being felled. While all the ships that had not been blown aground were headed for safe ports, we were eighteen miles out at sea, unaware that we were the only ones still out there.

'Good morning to you, Steve,' Peter called out as he banged the door. 'Time to get up. And by the way, it's a trifle rough this morning.'

It was still dark as I got up. I could feel the ship moving roughly beneath me and could hear a loud moaning coming from the tower. When I got onto the bridge, an unbelievable sight met my eyes. Everything outside was white. Flying foam filled the air, reaching higher than the top of the ship's bridge. Visibility was down to about three yards. We couldn't even see the tower from the bridge, just blue flashes through the white as the foam caused the thousands of watts of broadcast power to arc and flash. Incredibly, the equipment seemed to be OK, and both Caroline and Monique were on the air as usual.

Going into the newsroom, I turned on the TV to get the first reports of the day from teletext. Nothing but static on all channels. I assumed that the TV aerial on the roof of the bridge had been torn away by the storm; I never guessed that all of Kent's TV transmitters had been forced off the air. I turned to the radio. The dial was silent: nothing where local station Invicta should have been, nothing at Radio 1.

I finally got Radio 4 – and listened with amazement to what they described as an emergency broadcast from the Met Office. The weatherman was explaining that they were only on air thanks to emergency generators, as all power supplies in London had been disrupted. He described the hurricane-force winds from the south-west, and this was followed by the travel news, which was basically a warning from the police not to travel. All trains were cancelled, all roads to London – and hundreds of minor roads in Kent – were blocked, and the police were advising everyone to stay indoors.

I was amazed: the *Ross Revenge* was behaving no more badly than it had in the last storm and, in fact, was not rolling too much. The fact that the winds were south-westerly helped, as there was land on that side of us – the only direction from which we had any protection.

Gradually, as dawn came, we were able to see a little way through the foam. Towering waves rolled majestically past us, but left us relatively unscathed. Mike pointed out that the wind was so fierce that it was actually holding the ship face into it, thus preventing us from turning to catch the waves broadside, which would have been disastrous for us. The ship was actually leaning backwards slightly with the force of the wind. 'Something will go soon – you mark my words,' Mike said.

The breakfast show that morning was great fun, if a little difficult: we knew we were one of very few radio stations which had managed to stay on air during the storm. The storm itself was the major news item, of course, and Peter made great play on air of just how rough things were out at the Falls Head, at one stage describing the scene outside the studio porthole as 'a seething cauldron of saline hostility'.

Caroline's studio, Studio 1, was the best to be in during a storm, as it was in the exact centre of the ship. The Dutch next door in Studio 2 were having a hard time of it, however. Their records and equipment were flying all over the place – mainly because they always left stuff in messy piles. Over on Caroline 558, it was business as usual.

Just before I was due to read the 7.30 news headlines, something caught my eye through the newsroom porthole. I looked out and saw with horror that part of our aerial feeder system had come loose from the mast and was swinging back and forth, with spectacular flashes of power appearing whenever it touched the metal mast or stays. This was serious. I ran to find Mike, told him to look at it, and ran back upstairs, arriving, panting, in the newsroom just as Peter opened the news-mike for me to read the headlines. I grabbed my piece of paper and read the headlines, and Peter asked on-air if I'd been running a marathon. I told him, and the listeners, that I'd been running around the ship frantically trying to locate our engineer, as we seemed to have a problem with our aerial.

'Ah . . . . Let's hope its not too serious,' Peter said, before announcing the next record.

Peter soon broke in over the record, though, and announced that our engineer had told him that we had a problem with our aerial and were shutting down immediately. There was a sound of running footsteps as people arrived on the bridge to assess the situation. Mike arrived back from the transmitter room and explained that not only had one of the thick metal stays on the mast snapped but that it had ripped away some old disused aerial feeder cable with it. Both of these three-hundred-foot-long pieces of metal were now flailing about, wrapping themselves around everything else. They were shorting out the power from the transmitter and might snag the main aerial feeder cables. Something had to be done straight away.

We looked out of the windows. The sea was mountainous, the spray still flying through the air. It would be suicidal to attempt any maintenance work on the mast in the middle of this hurricane. But it had to be done; otherwise, we could be off the air for days.

Peter, who moments before had been safely ensconced in a warm studio, lost no time in acting to save the situation. 'Well, it's madness to try and climb the tower,' he announced, 'but I think I can reach the wires and catch them from the top of the bridge, and then tie them back so they do no more damage. What do you think, Mike?'

Mike looked at the swirling maelstrom outside and shrugged. 'OK, let's do it,' he replied. All the rest of us could do was help kit the two brave men out in waterproof gear and organise some hot soup for when they returned – *if* they returned.

When they opened the bridge doors to go outside, the howling of the wind increased tenfold, and we could almost taste the white spray hurling past. They went out, and within seconds were lost from sight. We could hear them moving around on the bridge roof, and waited anxiously. They eventually managed to tie the piece back. They returned indoors looking like two Arctic explorers who had been lost for months. Mike went straight down to the transmitter room to switch us back on, and Peter went back to the studio to resume the breakfast show. We were on air again at 8.20; incredibly, we had been off air for less than an hour. Somehow, nothing seemed too much effort to keep Caroline on the air.

Peter coped admirably with the rest of his breakfast show, despite the fact that he was still in his waterproof gear, and dripping everywhere. At 10 AM, Chris came on to relieve him. Peter decided to go back to bed; I couldn't say I blamed him. At 10.30, another stay snapped on the mast, and once again urgent work was needed to remedy the situation. I didn't think it was fair to wake Peter up again, so this time I volunteered to go outside with Mike. Now it was my turn to brave the hurricane. This time, there was an added complication: the station was staying on air, as Mike had had difficulty firing up the transmitter after the last break. As long as we were on the air, the transmitter would stay on, but if it was turned off again, Mike was afraid that we would be 'off' until the storm was over. We would just have to be careful up on the roof not to get too close to the live aerial cables, and not to touch the stay when it made contact with the aerial – at which point it would be carrying 50 kilowatts of power.

Outside was a screaming nightmare of wind and spray which took my breath away. Climbing up the ladder on to the roof was terrifying: the ship bucked and rolled as if it was trying to shake us off. I held on tightly, and made it to the roof, where I was exposed to the full force of the hundred-mile-an-hour winds. Mike and I clung on to each other and wedged ourselves up against a railing near the funnel, so that at least the wind was pressing us up against something solid.

It took ages for us to catch the rogue stay, which was swinging back and forth through the air with deadly force, occasionally coming into contact with the aerial and glowing blue. All the time, we were almost blinded by spray and were constantly in danger of being tipped over the side into the sea, thirty feet below.

Finally, we managed to catch the stay as it came past, though the force of it almost sent us crashing into the tower. We clung on to it for dear life to steady ourselves, then quickly tied it back against the ship's superstructure using some metal wire. That would hold it for the time being, at least. When we had finished, we looked up at the gigantic mast towering above us. Spray had been carried by the wind hundreds of feet up in the air, almost to the top of the mast, and dozens of the porcelain insulators used on the metal stays were glowing and crackling blue as the water hit them, shorting out our broadcast power.

'We're going to have more than a few broken stays to deal with after this!' Mike yelled at me through the wind. 'That whole lot is going to have to be checked out inch by inch. It's a miracle we're still on the air at all.'

Eventually we made it back indoors, and then it was down to the galley for a welcome cup of tea and a chance to dry off. Even down in the mess room, the moaning of the wind in the tower was quite loud, almost drowning out the sound of Caroline coming from the speaker on the wall.

By midday, the TV stations were coming back on air again, so I was able to get plenty of details from teletext for my one o'clock news, then settled down to watch the TV news, with its pictures of the devastation. After a while, I was disturbed by a strange grinding noise, which seemed to occur at irregular intervals and to come from above my head. I listened for ages, trying to figure out what it could be, and noticed that whenever it occurred, the TV picture broke up as well. I finally placed it as coming from outside and above me – it must be the tower. Dashing outside, I braved the wind once more to climb up on to the bridge roof, and hung on as best I could, waiting to see if I could spot what was wrong. The stays we had tied back earlier were still secure, and nothing else seemed to be loose. Just then, I heard the noise again and saw a shower of blue sparks coming off the mast, about a third of the way up. I watched again, and then saw it happen

— a single high-voltage cable had come loose and, as the ship rolled in the swell, it would come into contact with the metal tower and make the whole structure live. When this happened, the whole of our broadcast signal would be shorting away. It must sound to listeners as though we were constantly going off the air for a few seconds, then coming on again. I hastened down to the engineer's cabin and woke Mike.

We closed down straight away and got Peter Phillips out of bed to survey the situation. The storm had died down considerably by now, but it was still quite rough, so it was decided that we would clean up on deck for a couple of hours before attempting to climb the tower. The whole deck of the *Ross* was littered with seaweed and chunks of wood and other debris, which normally floated by on the sea, but which had been hurled at us by the wind. Apparently nothing like this had ever occurred before on the *Ross Revenge*. It took six of us two hours just to clear the seaweed and flotsam from the various outside decks of the ship, by which time the winds had died down to virtually nothing, the sea had become less swollen, and a weak sun was shining in the sky. Peter and Mike donned their climbing gear and set off up the tower: Mike concentrated on repairs to the lower sections, while Peter climbed the full three hundred feet to the top and began to work his way down. It must have been terrifying for Peter, three hundred feet up in the air at the top of that mast, as the ship was still moving from side to side. We could barely see him, way above our heads.

The two men put new stays on to replace the broken ones, replaced some insulators which had burned through, and repaired some damage to the aerial at the top, where it had become tangled. Mike sent a message to land via Chicago's emergency system, saying that the mast had been tremendously stressed by the hurricane, and that it was essential that a team of riggers and welders visited us as soon as possible to inspect for metal fatigue or cracks. Finally, at 11.30 PM, we came back on the air, with a short broadcast from Peter reassuring listeners that the ship had survived the big storm in one piece and that the station would be on the air the following morning as normal. They then turned the transmitters off for some further work: for once, I got to sleep the entire night.

The next day, the ship got back to a state of shattered normality. Everybody was drained from the exertions of the previous day. The promised English tender finally arrived on Tuesday – not the usual fishing boat from Ramsgate, but a larger one called the *Eileen*, captained by a man called Sammy.

Within ten minutes of the *Eileen* arriving, it had left again, after hurriedly giving us supplies and staff. What we did not know, however, was that Sammy had been paid a substantial extra sum to stay alongside the *Ross* for a few hours, because also on board the *Eileen* had been the rigger and welder sent out by Cosmic to inspect the tower and do any repairs necessary following the hurricane. The tender came and went so quickly that we never even found out that these people had been on board and willing to do the job

In a further twist of fate, the rigger broke his leg within hours of returning to land, and forgot to ring Cosmic to tell him that the survey of the mast for structural damage had not taken place. So Cosmic and Ronan were now quite happy, believing that the job had been done, and out on the ship we were still assuming that the surveyors would arrive out sometime soon. The only person who knew what had happened was the tender-skipper Sammy, who just took our extra money and buggered off.

We welcomed on board the considerable influx of new staff, which promised to end the double-shifting and extra hours that we had had for the last month. There were four DJs: Jackie Lee and Simon West returning, along with a new recruit, Pat Brooks, and a man called Nigel Harris, who had been on both the *Ross* and the *Mi Amigo* many years before.

This meant that for the first time in many months we could run Caroline twenty-four hours a day, seven days a week, without me having to do anything other than my normal news-shift. I was sad to lose my programmes but glad that I'd be able to put more effort into running the newsroom again.

As well as the on-air crew, there was an old seaman by the name of Ernie, a marine engineer who had worked on the *Ross Revenge* in the sixties when it was a fish-factory ship! He knew the workings of the vessel inside out and would help Mike get it in tip-top shape for the winter. Ernie was a treasure, with his broad north-of-England accent, and tales of life at sea on the *Ross* in the 'good old days' when she was fishing off the Icelandic coast. With a crew of twelve aboard (six English DJs, a newsreader, an engineer, a marine engineer and three Dutch), there were more than enough hands to do all the work. Things were going just fine.

The days went by, enlivened by the attentions of a friendly captain on one of the Olau Line ferries, who sailed his ship as close to us as he dared every time he passed by. On one occasion, his ferry passed so close to us that he was able to throw some onions on to the back deck of the Ross, having discovered through conversations with us on the ship-to-shore radio that we were in need of some. He suggested that the coming weekend, he could stop and drop anchor nearby, and we could come across and visit him in our little inflatable boat. We were thrilled at the idea of something so out of the ordinary.

On the Saturday, the wind died down to nothing, the sea became as calm as a millpond, and even the clouds drifted away, letting the moon shine down and light the sea all around for us. Eventually the *Olau Britannia* could be seen heading towards us, lit up like a Christmas tree. We went out on deck and started manhandling the rubber boat out of its cradle, and lowering it into the water. We cast off from the *Ross* and headed out across to the ferry, which towered over us like a block of flats.

The ferry captain shone his ship's searchlight down on us, and we could see curious passengers peering out of the windows above – doubtless wondering why their cross-channel ferry had decided to stop in the middle of nowhere at midnight to meet with four odd-looking people in a tiny boat. The captain and crew appeared twenty or thirty feet up, peering over the side and shouting greetings to us.

On board, we were made very welcome. The crew sent down a bucket on the end of a rope, containing packages for all of us. It became apparent that most of the crew had chipped in to buy their friends from the radio ship something: bottles of wine and spirits, chocolates and sweets, magazines, books and fresh vegetables. We thanked them and then, reluctantly, started to pull away. However, just as we were pulling away from the *Britannia*, the steering cable on our little craft snapped. Suddenly we were ploughing through the water, out of control, going round and round in circles, the ferry's spotlight trained on us. We almost crashed into the side of the ferry at full speed, then Mike cut the engine, and we started drifting, while he tried to sort out the steering. We drifted down along the side of the ferry, and then right in behind the stern, out of sight of its crew. That was really terrifying – the *Britannia* was towering above us, and if it had started its engines at that moment, we would have been swept out of the boat and sucked into its propellers.

After a tense few minutes, Mike managed to make a temporary repair, and we started the engine and got clear of the danger zone. We all quietly breathed a sigh of relief that we had an engineer with us, who regularly managed to patch things up and keep Caroline on the air, who was willing to do extra hours on air as well as working on engines, who had brought us safely through the hurricane, and who had now saved us yet again from an embarrassing and possibly dangerous situation. We waved goodbye to our friends on the ferry, and turned around, pointing our little boat at the *Ross Revenge* to head for home – and caught our breath in wonder.

The moon shining down from a cloudless sky had turned the sea into a pool of dancing light, and we were chugging our way through what seemed like liquid silver. A million points of light winked at us on the silver sea. And there, sitting serene and proud in the centre of this wonder, was the *Ross Revenge*, its lights twinkling, the tower reaching up into the sky, seeming to pierce the moon in the very centre.

Time stood still, and no one spoke or made a sound as we slid through the water towards this apparition. We all just stared at this beautiful vessel that was our home, our jobs, our lives – our whole world as long as we were at sea.

There, behind those lights, was everything we possessed, all our achievements as well as all our hopes and dreams, free out here, beyond the reach of any government. The giant mast that towered into the sky reached out and touched millions of people around Europe with its invisible vibrations, sending its message of love and good music to a hundred cities and a thousand towns.

The moment seemed to last for an eternity, and then, suddenly, we were alongside the *Ross*, and friendly hands were reaching down to help us climb back on board. Taking one last look at the *Ross* as seen from outside, I climbed back up, then started helping to unload the rubber boat and bring it back on board.

Afterwards, I wandered around out on deck for a while, then sat right up on the bow of the ship, washed in moonlight, letting the silver sea fill my vision.

6

THE FALL

NOVEMBER 1987

Chicago, meanwhile, had started work on a new project: converting the spare medium-wave transmitter into a short-wave one, capable of covering the whole of Europe. This would allow us to run a third station with religious programmes on twenty-four hours a day and, consequently, generate greater revenue for Caroline. Chicago warned us to stay away from the transmitter room, as he had constructed a temporary aerial to do some tests with. Because there were no insulators to carry it through the deck, the aerial came up the transmitter-room stairs and out to the mast that way. Whenever Chicago was testing his creation, there were thousands of volts going through the aerial wire – making it very dangerous to attempt to go down the stairs.

As we continued into November, there was an increasing feeling of excitement on board the Caroline ship. The new short-wave station would be launching soon, and plans were afoot for further developments, with a new, bigger transmitter on order for 558, and the possibility of the old one being used to start a third medium-wave service, running country music and religion.

Everywhere you went on board, new items were being installed, work was being done, and empty rooms were being cleared out for use as new studios and library facilities. Money was also being heavily invested in our Caroline 558 service by the company behind the Canadian lottery advertising, who had seen great results in terms of ticket sales following our increase in power, and who wanted to improve the quality on 558 even more.

I found myself dragged into doing all kinds of interesting work, sometimes in far-flung parts of the ship I had barely visited before. Mike himself worked non-stop in those days, installing equipment, surveying empty rooms for possible conversion to studios, dragging things around, testing and adjusting our new short-wave transmitter, in addition to all his usual tasks of running and maintaining the ship and generators. Sometimes he would work for seventy-two hours and then collapse into his cabin, unwakeable for twenty-four hours or more

Just to add extra spice to our life, it was a particularly good month for chart music: 'China In Your Hand' by T'Pau, 'Crazy Crazy Nights' by Kiss, 'Here I Go Again' by Whitesnake, 'Satellite' by the Hooters, and many more. These, coupled with our excellent back catalogue and the buzzing atmosphere of the *Ross Revenge*, meant that I really enjoyed my programmes on those wild November nights.

However good it was on the ship, I knew I would have to take a break on land soon, as the rent I had prepaid for my flat had long since been used up, and I would need to sort matters out. Mid-November came, and with it a brief spell of flat calm weather, and one night I got the knock on my cabin door that I had been expecting.

'Ah . . . Steve,' said Peter Phillips, coming into my cabin and switching on the light. 'Sorry to wake you at this early hour, but there's a small English tender here, and I'll be going off on it. I just wondered if you wanted to come off as well, or stay on for another few weeks?'

'You know what my answer to that is,' I said, jumping out of bed and beginning to dress rapidly. 'I'll see you upstairs in a minute.'

It was 4 AM and bitterly cold, and I emerged out on deck to see a small Ramsgate fishing boat, the *FourWinds*, bobbing about in the water. Kevin was clambering aboard, accompanied by my brother Chris. Kevin greeted me warmly and explained that he'd like me to stay on for a while but that, as I'd been out here for so long, he would understand if I wanted to go. I was quite tempted to stay on for another few weeks, as by now I was very caught up in the excitement of everything that was going on. Kevin passed on some mail for me, which I opened. There was a letter from Surbiton, telling me my land-lady was going to throw all my possessions out if I didn't collect them soon. I reluctantly told Kevin that I had to come off after all.

Just before we got off the ship, Peter buttonholed Kevin, asking him why it was taking the office so long to send out a rigger and welder when the mast was obviously in need of inspection after the hurri-cane. It was then that both parties discovered what had happened when the *Eileen* had visited us, and how the office had believed that the mast was now inspected and safe. Peter said he would take the matter up with Ronan at once. I felt a real wrench as we pulled away in the *FourWinds*, knowing that what we were leaving behind was my only home now. I wondered just what lay ahead of me on land, and whether coming off had in fact been the right thing to do. I made a quick cal-culation in my head – my stint had lasted a hundred and one days; a long time to spend out at sea. As we pulled away, I spotted something bright and flickering high up on the mast. One of the insulators on an important side stay was arcing and burning in the morning mist. I pointed it out to Peter, and he nodded in grim determination. My last sight of the ship and the mast as we chugged away from the Falls Head that morning was that arcing insulator, burning high up in the sky like a brand new star.

After we reached London Victoria, we parted to go our separate ways, I phoned John Burch, who said that he and his wife Anita would be happy to put me up for a few days.

John and Anita were extremely kind to me, and allowed me un-limited use of their home and all its facilities for as long as I needed it. I didn't want to overstay my welcome, however, so did my best to get in touch with Cosmic via a phone number that John had given me for the business premises of his friend Peter Moore, whom Cosmic appar-ently visited often. There was no reply to any of the messages that I left for him, and eventually I became quite worried because my money had virtually run out. I decided to trek across London to where Moore ran his business, a carburettor centre near Highgate, to hang around there and perhaps run into Cosmic face to face.

Reaching Moore's premises, which were on both sides of a busy main road, beside a pub called the Black Rose, I was pleased to find a big open fire in the main office, where I warmed myself while waiting for someone to appear. Peter Moore, 'PM', eventually arrived, having been in the pub for lunch, and greeted me warmly, offering me some money out of his till so that I could go and get lunch myself. He was a thin man, middle-aged, with the long hair and friendly face of a happy hippie. He told me that Cosmic was away at the moment and that he was fulfilling Cosmic's duties for now.

A little later, Ronan phoned and asked me to meet him at a restaurant called the Picasso, half way along the King's Road in Chelsea. He had something he wanted to discuss with me there, and he also had some money for me. PM said I could spend the night in his flat, which was a couple of doors down the road from the office, and directly opposite another office and yard that he owned.

The next day, bright and early, I took a number 11 bus to the King's Road, and walked up the street until I located the Picasso, an Italian restaurant. I took my place at an empty table, ordered a cappuccino and waited.

'Hey Stevie Baby. Good to see you,' Ronan said as he strode into the restaurant twenty minutes late. 'Do you want to eat?'

He ordered breakfast for us both, looked around cagily, lowered his head conspiratorially and asked me to put a hand under the table towards his knee. I was puzzled, but did as I was told. I found his hand under the table and was surprised to have a thick bundle of banknotes pressed into my hands.

'That's just for starters,' he said in a low voice. 'If you need more, tell me later, but don't count it here – the walls have eyes.'

'Honestly,' I said. 'Anybody who saw us would think you were a dirty old man paying off a rent-boy.'

I had known that Ronan was paranoid about security but was unprepared for the vetting he gave me for half an hour before he would even talk about the ship. At one stage, he even suggested that I might be in the Irish Secret Service.

'Don't be silly,' I said. 'There *is* no Irish Secret Service.'

'That's what makes them so dangerous,' Ronan replied cagily. 'They're so secret that no one knows about them.'

This then got him talking about one of his favourite subjects – the Kennedy assassination and it was a full hour before he finally got on to the subject of the ship. He told me what it was he wanted to talk to me about.

He said that, as Cosmic was leaving the organisation due to personal problems and with Tom Anderson having also recently left, he needed someone to help PM for a few weeks on land.

Ronan arranged transport for me, in the form of a very elderly Transit van, and I spent the next week running various errands for the station while staying in a spare room at Peter's Highgate flat. After my first full week helping Peter, I went to see Ronan again, and he handed me a list of requirements that our marine engineer Ernie had sent, together with £300 to pay for them, and some more money to keep myself fed and the van rolling. We also agreed that a major priority for the next tender must be a team of riggers and welders to examine the mast – though with the November weather being almost constantly rough, we had no idea when that would be. Meanwhile, he was meeting potential new Dutch backers with the possibility of them investing in the ship. In preparation for the deal, the Dutch service was changing frequency from 963 to 819 kHz: a new high power transmitter located in Finland had recently switched on, and was considerably reducing our range after dark, affecting both Monique and the Viewpoint religious service – and Caroline's revenues.

The next week, I got several pieces of good news. Jane from Laser called and told me that one of her old record-plugging contacts from Laser had come through, and wanted to pay several thousands pounds for a plugging deal with Caroline. Normally our record plugs were for small companies, but this was one of the biggest labels. A chap called Mango, another advertising and plug salesman, phoned the carburettor centre that afternoon, telling me he had just negotiated a deal worth tens of thousands of pounds for us to advertise holidays to a particular Caribbean country, the government of the country in question being the ones who would pay us.

Later that evening, driving through north London on an errand for PM, I had Caroline on the radio and it was sounding good. Tim Allen was on the air, and he was playing song after song that I really liked. The signal was rock-solid, even though it was medium wave, at night, in winter. I thought about all the plans which were now going ahead to make Caroline even more powerful and profitable during the coming months, and about the new advertisers, plug records and staff that would soon be going on air.

On the radio, Tim was commenting that they were in the middle of a strong north-easterly gale, with ferociously rough seas, and that the ship was rolling from side to side. I knew what that situation was like. Then another great song came on, and I drove on, tapping the steering wheel to the rhythm of the music. Things were great; we were really going places. I reached my destination, turned off the radio and went indoors.

And later, at 3.50 AM in the middle of that cold November night, out at the Falls Head, one insulator too many glowed cherry red and shattered under the stress, one stay too many on the giant mast was loosened as a result . . . Then the stays loosened and flapped in the teeth of the gale, and snapped, one by one, as the entire three hundred feet of metal came twisting and crashing down out of the sky, smashing everything that stood in its path, ripping railings and equipment right down to the bottom of the transmitter room, and the whole lot – mast, stays and aerials – disappeared into the icy blackness of the North Sea, taking the station of our dreams with it.

The ship was still afloat, but it was bare as a rock on the storm-tossed sea, and the north-easterly winds howled in triumph through the mastless sky.

The *Ross Revenge* with the original three-hundred-foot tall mast
(Photo: Steve Conway)

Stays supporting the broadcast tower   (Photo: Steve Conway)

The ship in 1988, with the new twin masts built at sea. The front mast is partially made from cod-liver oil piping.   (Photo: CM Archives)

Steve Conway in the Caroline news room on the *Ross Revenge*
(Photo: Chris Kennedy)

Left to right: Kevin Turner, Mike Watts, Chris Kennedy and Ernie
Stevenson in the galley in November 1987 (Photo: Jeanette Pearson)

Peter Chicago at the transmitter room hatchway
(Photo: Jeanette Pearson)

Left to right: Dave Richards, Steve Masters (behind), Steve Conway, Neil Gates and Nigel Harris at a Caroline Movement event in London
(Photo: Geoff Baldwin)

Ronan O'Rahilly and Tom Anderson
(Photo: Peter Messingfield)

John Burch and Peter Moore plot over a pint.
(Photo: Peter Messingfield)

Coconut in the 558 studio. The 'format clocks' for music playlisting can be seen on either side of the studio clock (Photo: John Burch)

The record library with its thousands of LPs and singles
(Photo: John Burch)

Steve Conway and John Burch at a Caroline Movement rally in London following the Dutch government's raid on the ship in 1989

(Photo: CM Archives)

Smuggling new mast sections to the coast on an open-top sightseeing bus

(Photo: Steve Taplin)

The North Sea in winter was a bleak and stormy place, particularly when gales came from the north or north-east. These dramatic photos taken by Paul Shelton show the *Ross Revenge* in stormy weather in 1988.

7

Faith No More

NOVEMBER–DECEMBER 1987

'Wake up!' PM was shaking me. 'The ship's off the air, and I think they have a problem with the mast.'

I woke suddenly, feeling the urgency in his words. PM was half-dressed and looking worried.

'I woke up early and found that the station was off the air,' he explained, 'so then I tuned into Invicta Radio and they said on the news that the *Ross Revenge* was in trouble. They said that the main transmitter had fallen overboard. I guess they must mean the mast.'

The two of us sat in the front room of the flat for a while, wondering how we could get more information. I hit on the idea of phoning Dover coastguard, saying that I was the brother of a crew-member and that I wanted to know if everything was all right. I wouldn't be lying, as Chris was out there, but I wouldn't be telling them that I actually worked for the station either. Dover coastguard would not give information out normally, and of course would not handle ship-to-shore telephone calls to a pirate ship, but they might give information to an anxious relative. The coastguard confirmed our fears. The Invicta news report had been right – the *Ross Revenge*'s mast had collapsed and fallen overboard and the storm had caused other damage to the ship. But on the plus side, everybody was all right on board, and there was no real danger to the vessel.

I phoned Carol Chicago, to see if she could get a message through to the ship on Chicago's emergency radio link. The aerial for this was a third of the way up the mast, so if only part of it had collapsed, the link would still work. We desperately needed to contact the ship, to find out how bad the damage was, and what materials needed to be shipped out to repair or rebuild the broadcast tower.

Carol was in tears, she had heard the news reports and was naturally extremely worried about her husband. She was relieved to hear that the coastguard had told me that everyone was safe, but told me that she had tried to contact the ship, to no avail. She read me a message which Chicago had been sending from the ship via a telex machine over his radio link during the night – a message that had cut off abruptly, possibly when the disaster had happened. It read: 'Conditions very rough out here. Off air with aerial problems. Some stays loose on mast – everything . . .'

The time of the message was 3.50 AM. According to the telex machine at Chicago's house, the transmission had cut off mid-message. Despite numerous attempts, contact with the ship after that had not been re-established. Obviously, even Chicago's emergency radio system was in ruins.

I thanked Carol, promised to call her again when I had more news, and started calling around to mobilise support. Mike Watts initially cursed me for waking him so early, but once he had heard what had happened, agreed to come straight to London for a crisis conference. Then I called anyone else I thought could be of help, including all the regular crew members who were on shore.

When the hour was more civilised, I telephoned the families of the crew out on the ship so that they would know that their sons, husbands or boyfriends were safe. Shortly after 10 AM, Ronan rang. He had been alerted to the silence of the ship by the Dutch businessmen with whom he had just concluded a deal to sell the airtime currently being used by Monique.

'I'll tell them it's off the air for generator repairs until we can find out how quickly we can get back on the air,' he told me on the phone. 'Let's face it, if we have to rebuild that baby at sea, we're going to need all the dough we can get, and we don't want to spook them before we know exactly what the situation is.'

Never had the *Ross Revenge* seemed so far from land – we desperately needed information before we could even start to plan ahead, and doubtless the people on the ship desperately needed to talk to us as well. PM and I waited eagerly for Bill in Essex, our CB man, to make his regular scheduled call to the ship, and then phone us with the news.

We gathered in the pub and, at 6 PM, regular as clockwork, Bill phoned and told us the worst. Of the three hundred feet of broadcast tower, there were just three inches left. Three inches! It had snapped off clean at the base, and gone straight overboard. It was a miracle that no one had been hurt. Bill concluded with the obvious news that a tender was urgently required. Chicago had a list of engineering requirements as long as his arm, but even if these were met, the ship would still be far from ready to broadcast again. And the north-easterly was still blowing strong, with mountainous seas, so we couldn't get a boat out to the *Ross* yet. Ronan phoned soon afterwards and was told the news. Even his usual optimism was dented by what he heard, but he requested that Mike Watts and I meet him on the King's Road at midday the following day. He said that he had swung the deal with the Dutch and that we would have to work hard to get Caroline back on the air somehow, as well as to secure a second service for the Dutch.

Ronan's optimism infected us, and we were slightly happier as we sat in the pub, but we still had no illusions about the task ahead of us. It was the middle of winter and we had to buy, transport and build a new tower and aerial system on a ship that was badly damaged and was no longer bringing in money.

The following morning, over breakfast, I held a mini-conference with PM and Mike Watts. The North Sea was still in the grip of strong north-easterly gales, so there was no hope of us organising a tender. All we could do for the moment was liaise with Ronan, draw up a hit-list of emergency supplies and wait. We decided to have the *Bellatrix* standing by for when the weather calmed down. I phoned Freddie Bolland in Holland from PM's flat, but was shocked at his response. Freddie informed me that since he had now sold his interest in Monique to another group, via Ronan, and since Monique was now, in any case, off the air and in ruins, he would not be willing to run the *Bellatrix* out to the Falls Head to help us. As far as he was concerned, the Dutch crew he had put on board were no longer his responsibility, nor was he obliged to run any tenders for us.

Through the morning and in the days that followed, people continued to phone or drop in to the carburettor centre to commiserate or offer moral support. Some were people I had worked with, like Tom Anderson, who phoned to express his shock, or John Tyler, who popped in briefly to share memories of his stint on Caroline and the times he had climbed the big tower.

With the exception of Tom, most of those calling in were very bleak in their assessment of Caroline's future now that the three-hundred-foot mast had collapsed. Most expected it to mark the end of the station on the *Ross Revenge*, perhaps for good. In their view it would be simply impossible to rebuild the mast while the ship was at sea, and any attempt to put into a European port for repairs would see the ship impounded and its crew arrested.

'It's over'; 'It was great while it lasted'; 'It will never be the same again'; 'The kindest thing would be just to bring the ship in and call it a day, it's never going to last now it's way out at the Falls Head.' So many people were telling us that this was it and we should just give up.

We couldn't let this happen. I wasn't going to write Caroline off as a lost cause and walk away, and neither was PM. Mike Watts was full of ideas for how the broadcast antennae could be rebuilt from scratch, but it would need a large amount of supplies – and a lot of money. Talking to Ronan was a top priority – he had been busy with the Dutch businessmen, but was now free to see us in the afternoon.

Mike and I set off for Chelsea, stepping off the platform of the bus onto the King's Road at exactly noon, a blast of the cold north-easterly wind in our faces before we managed to dash inside the meeting-place, a very fashionable eatery known by us as the 'Pancake HQ', though the sign above the door proclaimed it to be 'The Veritable Crêperie'.

We were ushered downstairs, where Ronan sat in almost regal splendour at a table meant for six.

'Hey, Mike, Stevie Baby, how'ya doing?'

'Not too well really,' Mike replied, 'but perhaps you can help us.'

We ordered coffee and pancakes, and got down to business. For the first time in more than twenty-four hours, a little gleam of hope entered my mind. Ronan would not give up. His ability to sort out even the toughest of scrapes was legendary and, of course, he had been through all this mast-collapse business many times before, with the old Caroline ship, the *Mi Amigo*, in the seventies. We sat with him for four hours, gradually working out a plan to get Caroline back on the air again, on low power in the short term, and to bring back a full service, including the Dutch stations, by Christmas.

Money was still coming in to the station for religion and airtime sales for the previous month, but this would soon dry up, and it was obviously crucial that we get something back on the air as soon as possible. Ronan explained that even the most low-powered of temporary signals would help in the short term, because it would enable him to convince investors and the Dutch that we were getting things back together again. To this end, Mike and I were to take the van, and visit as many radio-equipment suppliers as possible, to get together whatever Chicago needed to get the station back on the air on a temporary basis. While doing this, we could also source out the mast sections and the bulk of supplies that would be needed later to restore the broadcast installation to its former glory.

There, between the three of us, we designed the structure for the *Ross*'s new aerial system, drawing it in biro on a paper napkin. Using only this rough drawing, and mental calculations, Mike was able to design a new tower and aerial array that would have to last us for at least a year. Over rounds of pancakes, and numerous cups of coffee, we worked feverishly through the afternoon, planning not only the form that the new antenna system would take, but how to source and transport the huge and expensive list of components that Mike said were needed to construct it.

Building a new three-hundred-foot tower at sea in winter was out of the question, so Mike designed a system using two 120-foot towers; one at either end of the ship, with a 'T'-shaped aerial strung between them, which he said would be almost as good. An aerial of the same design had been used by Laser in the early eighties, with very good results. Ronan watched Mike's plans being drawn, and then mentioned a Canadian firm that was apparently manufacturing a revolutionary type of new medium-wave broadcast aerial, made totally of fibreglass, which stood ninety feet tall on its own, without need of stays or mast. Mike cautioned against this, arguing that we did not have money to waste on untried equipment, and that Chicago, who was very much a traditionalist, would be against it anyway. Knowing how keen Ronan always was to throw vast sums of money at what he perceived to be technological wonders, Mike made him promise not to order such a system until he had at least discussed it fully with Chicago. We were then given a couple of thousand pounds in cash – slipped under the table as usual – for us to buy whatever was immediately needed and to pay for an English tender. We knew we would have several days to plan, as the weather was still rough.

The next day we went to Brighton, Mike's home town, where there were apparently a number of radio-supply places which might have what we needed. Before setting off, I phoned a major pirate radio station in Dublin, Sunshine Radio, and spoke to its owner, Robbie Dale. Explaining who I was, and what had happened to Caroline, I asked if I could say we were buying equipment for Sunshine, in case we were asked any awkward questions. Buying radio equipment for Caroline was, of course, illegal, but if we were buyers for a foreign pirate, no one would care less and we would be less likely to be reported to the DTI by a suspicious retailer. Robbie, who had worked for Caroline himself in the sixties, readily agreed to the deception, commenting that anything he could do to help Caroline was no trouble at all.

So, as we set off for the south coast, we rehearsed our new identities. I was Robbie's right-hand man, buying equipment for his station in Ireland, and Mike was the English engineer contracted to install it. After visits to several different places, Mike directed me to a second-hand radio-equipment business, run from an old run-down farmhouse, set in acres of overgrown land, at the end of a tiny country lane.

We immediately knew that we had come to the right place. Sections of tower of varying sizes and lengths lay all over the place in the long grass, there were piles of insulators everywhere, and under cover in the old farm sheds was a virtual Aladdin's cave of spare parts and cables for high-power transmission. Most of the stuff was government surplus – ex-Ministry of Defence, mainly. The place was run by an old man called Bill, who guessed from the sort of equipment we were looking at, and the money we were spending, that we were working on a big installation. He seemed to accept our story that the equipment was all going to an Irish pirate.

We spent the afternoon negotiating prices, and eventually the van was loaded up with insulators, copper wire, radio valves and electronic equipment – with some scaffold poles thrown in for good measure. More importantly, we had our eye on a huge pile of metal tower sections lying in a corner of Bill's field, which Mike suggested would be very suitable for our longer-term plans. We negotiated a price and agreed to purchase them later, subject to Chicago and Ronan's approval.

The following morning Peter and I set to work planning the tender that would deliver all this equipment to the *Ross*. The weather was still very rough, but it was meant to calm down for a few hours on Monday, so I rang our English tender skipper, Dave the Fish, and booked him for Monday night.

I then phoned around as many people as I could, trying to rustle up a replacement crew for the ship. With the exception of Tony Peters, who had already agreed to go out, no one wanted to know. All the people who had been so keen to go out to the Falls Head when Caroline was on the air did not want to help out now that times were tough. But I could appreciate that for many who saw Caroline simply as a pathway into jobs on the BBC or ILR (commercial radio) stations on land, going out to the ship when Caroline would in all probability remain off the air for an extended period was not only pointless but probably counterproductive.

I had a day of relative relaxation on Sunday, then Monday dawned, and it was all go to organise things for that night's tender. Despite last-minute calls by me, no one else was willing to go out: I would have to persuade most of those stuck out there to stay there for the time being. I decided that, if the situation was unchanged in a few weeks' time, I would have to go back out myself, leaving things on shore in PM's hands – despite the fact that he had a business to run himself and Cosmic did not look to be coming back.

The day went by in a flurry of activity and in the evening a large crowd of us jammed into the Transit van and a Volvo borrowed from PM for the journey down to Ramsgate. I would be going out and back to survey the ship and reassure the crew. Mike Watts was to make the return trip to talk to Chicago and discuss technical plans, and PM had lent me one of his employees, an Australian called Crocodile, to help us out. According to the weather report, conditions were now calm.

We arrived down in Ramsgate harbour at the appointed time, and waited in the darkness of a little-used section of quayside while Dave the Fish manoeuvred his boat alongside the steps. We struggled to get all the equipment out of the van and onto the fishing boat without attracting undue attention. A short while later, we chugged out of the harbour and headed out to sea, just like any other little fishing vessel on a night fishing trip. Dave told us that a big imbalance in numbers between people going out and coming in would look suspicious, so, as only one person was going out to the ship to stay, we could take off two crew members at the most.

All the way out on the fishing boat, we waited tensely to see what the *Ross Revenge* would look like when we eventually reached it. After nearly a week of hearing third-hand reports, we would soon see the damage for ourselves. Normally, the tower could be seen from miles away as a pencil-thin mark on the horizon. Even at night, its lights were clearly visible at the very top, but this time, even when we were well past the Drillstone buoy and heading towards international waters, we could see nothing. Dave the Fish pointed out glumly the echo of the *Ross* on his radar set – normally the brightest dot on the screen (the mast made a giant target for radar) it now looked small and dim.

Eventually the lights of the *Ross Revenge* came into sight, and she was revealed to be in a very bedraggled state. As we came around the stern to tie up alongside her starboard deck, we observed the torn railings, the battered metalwork, broken stays and shattered porcelain everywhere. The ship, which just a month before had been a proud vessel, was now listing heavily to one side.

There was none of the usual shouting and enthusiasm as we drew alongside. The DJs, the crew, even Chicago, looked pale and tired, depressed and, to a man, utterly defeated. The crew did not even raise a murmur when they were told that most of them would have to stay on board. They just looked even more gloomy, and asked me to make sure they all got off soon.

The biggest mess was where the tower had stood. Just a few inches of tangled and snapped metal now sprouted from the centre of the main deck, and there was a gaping hole where the feed-through insulator had plummeted thirty feet down into the transmitter room, smashing tens of thousands of pounds worth of delicate electronic equipment. Down in the transmitter room, the three transmitters themselves were all right, but so much damage had been done to the other equipment that it might take us months to rebuild it, even if we could afford to. The remains of the feed-through insulator, which had stood as tall as a Dalek, were all over the floor in a million pieces, intermingled with bits of the circuitry it had smashed.

When the mast had fallen, the dozens of stays had cut through the air like a giant egg-slicer. There were virtually no railings left anywhere on the ship and TV aerials, washing lines and Chicago's emergency radio aerial had all been pulverised. As the ship had been specially ballasted to compensate for the tall mast, the balance of the vessel was now all wrong, and we were told it now rolled around most violently in all but the calmest of weather. Also, the ship's rudder had apparently broken free from the steering gear and was banging violently against the hull as the ship rolled, making sleep all but impossible.

Chicago, for all his tired looks and pessimistic air, declared that he would do everything he could to put something on the air using the engineering supplies we had brought with us. It would not be very powerful or even sound very good, but it would show everyone that Caroline was on the road to recovery and, more importantly, would stake our claim to the much coveted 558 frequency. The BBC were known to want to use it for an Essex relay, and would possibly switch on if we were off the air too long.

Mike discussed tactics with Chicago, Crocodile heaved the new supplies on board, and I talked to the crew, trying to reassure them that our owner was going to buy a new mast and get it shipped out soon, and that I would run another tender to relieve them. Kevin Turner was first in the queue to leave, along with the new newsreader, Andrew, who had joined just before the tower fell down, and who had turned out to be very seasick. We pulled away from the *Ross* sometime after midnight, and chugged back towards land again.

A couple of days later I was back in Chelsea talking to Ronan, this time with Kevin Turner, instead of Mike, and planning what was needed for the next big tender. The money coming in to the station had now dried up, and Ronan was anxious that what he had left should not be wasted. He wanted me to organise another English tender, load it with enough food supplies to last until Christmas if necessary, and change over as many crew as possible. This way, with immediate needs taken care of, a large tender from France could bring out new mast sections and heavy lifting gear. As we would have to pay Freddie Bolland for this, it was obvious that unless we budgeted very carefully, we would end up staying off the air, broke.

I told Ronan that, if I couldn't get any new crew members, I would go out myself with Mike Watts and replace the entire crew if necessary, paying Dave the Fish extra to take off as many as he dared. Ronan approved, but said that the Dutch would have to stay on board until the special French tender ran, as it would be too risky to sneak foreign nationals into Ramsgate. PM would organise things from land, helped by Kevin, who told us that he was not interested in returning to the ship the time being.

Chicago was now able to use his emergency radio link to his house again, as we had brought out new parts for him on the tender. So we now had daily messages via his wife, which enabled us to plan things better.

And then, a couple of days later, a little miracle happened – Caroline came crackling back into life again, extremely weak and very low-powered, but broadcasting nonetheless. Chicago had cobbled together a tiny aerial array between the ship's funnel and its original short front mast (a little forty-foot mast from its fishing days). True, it could only be heard in east Kent, and then only during the daytime, but it was a start. The audio quality was terrible, as the lashed-up aerial was not tuned properly to 558 kHz, and even in Margate the signal was wobbly. Chicago had improvised, and used an upturned laundry basket for a feed-through insulator! Needless to say, this was entirely unsuitable, and the station went off the air every time it rained or the deck took on water from a wave.

By now, the community of dedicated Caroline fans had become aware of our plight, and offers were flooding in to John Burch and the Caroline Movement from people willing to donate food and materials to the ship, or help with organising or transporting materials on land. One couple had collected a considerable quantity of food and goodies for the ship, and these could go out on the next tender.

Another week flew by, with the sea rough again, and the crew reportedly more miserable than ever. PM and Kevin were now busy getting hold of the large items needed to build a proper aerial system, and I was ready to go back out to the ship. It was just a case of waiting once more for the weather to improve.

Peter Phillips was on holiday in America, and his absence at this time was keenly felt, as he was skilled in mast repairs and would have been able to advise us on materials needed for staying our new system. I had decided not to phone him in the USA to tell him the bad news, figuring that he might as well at least enjoy his holiday. He would be back at Christmas; in the meantime, now that it was back on the air, I would hold the fort as a deputy programme controller and DJ.

A couple of days before the next tender was planned, Ronan gave me £600 (a huge sum of money in 1987) to buy food for the ship. Chicago's wife, Carol, said that I could use her house and freezers for storing food until the weather was calm enough for the tender, and she offered to help with the shopping too. We spent £200 in her local butcher's, getting hundreds of cuts of meat, and then another £100 in the greengrocer's. Then it was off to Tesco's, where we bought a whole trolley-load of Christmas treats for the crew, as well as all the usual essentials. Staff in the store watched goggle-eyed when we eventually came to the checkouts with twelve fully laden trolleys, some of them stacked high with bread, long-life milk or sweets. 'Large family,' Carol explained to the checkout girl.

We took everything back to her house and then went out again – to buy hardware and other things for the vessel. We got five fan-heaters, new thicker blankets, and two dozen hot-water bottles. Then there was the bottled gas for cooking and heating – a mere twelve cylinders! At the end of the day, we had everything – even a Christmas tree.

Mike and I met Ronan in the Picasso and, over a very hearty meal, he wished us well on our stint. His girlfriend, Jenny, had gone on a record-buying spree, and he gave us a couple of hundred singles and albums – after all, Caroline was back on the air, even if it did only cover Kent.

With Caroline only on the air on 'peanut power', and very intermittently at that, virtually no one was willing to spend the winter on board – although we did have one volunteer, John Bibby, who was willing to join us as cook and general hand. We set off in the Transit van, packed full of Mike's next round of engineering purchases, and headed through a cold and frosty London for the M2 and the coast. We met John at Margate railway station; he had been driven there by a Caroline supporter from Reading, who stayed with us all afternoon helping us on the numerous runs from Chicago's house to Dave's boat in Ramsgate.

By 5 PM, we had all the equipment, food – and personnel – assembled on the quayside, and bang on time Dave the Fish appeared in his little boat to collect us. It took quite a while to load all the stuff on board, and when we had done so there was very little room for us, but we managed to squeeze on board and were soon chugging out to sea.

The *Ross Revenge* looked a little tidier when we reached it this time.

Chicago's temporary lashed-up aerial between the funnel and the front mast looked almost comical after our previous monster, but our situation was anything but comical. With the exception of my brother, everyone wanted off, even Tony Peters, who had only been there for ten days.

'You don't know how uncomfortable it is,' he told me. 'It's rolling like a pig in any sort of swell, and we're just tired of being thrown around all day long. It's as if the ship just doesn't want us any more and is trying to shake us off.'

Leaving us, apart from Chicago, were Tim Allen (who had been on board since before the hurricane – what a stint he must have had), Nigel Harris, Tony Peters, Keith Francis and Pat Brooks, as well as the marine engineer, Ernie Stevenson, who had been a great help during the crises – even managing to immobilise the loose rudder. In contrast to the heavily populated fishing boat, the *Ross* was now almost deserted – three Dutch, plus Chris, Mike, John Bibby and me.

I was now the programme controller of a radio station whose available broadcast staff consisted of just one DJ (my brother) and one newsreader (me). Well, this time there was no way I could avoid doing daytime programmes – even so, I'd still be short-staffed.

I went up to the 558 studio, deserted now, with the station off-air for the night, and started sorting out the music rotation, putting in some of the new single releases I had got from Ronan. Mike Watts joined me, and we worked out what I was going to do. Mike suggested that because, even in Margate and Ramsgate, reception faded out at night, we might as well just broadcast during daytime hours until the new towers were built and we were back on full power. He also told me that the newsroom could not be used at the moment, as the ship was so unstable now that the equipment had been stowed away for safety. He would have to rebuild the newsroom with everything bolted down, or fixed into the walls. This would, however, leave me free for my programme duties.

I decided to approach Wim De Walk, the one of the three Dutch DJs still on board, and offer him a programme on Caroline. This way, we would broadcast from 6 AM to 6 PM, with three four-hour shows, hosted by Chris, me and Wim. The Dutch, of course, had had no radio station since the mast had collapsed, and restoring a second frequency seemed a long way off: Wim eagerly agreed to my request. I had planned for Chris to do the breakfast show, but the following morning he was feeling ill, so I found myself not only on the air as a daytime DJ for the first ever time, but actually doing the breakfast show! It all seemed a far cry from my first day on the *Ross*, when I had been the bumbling new newsreader in Kevin Turner's breakfast show.

Although we were only covering a limited geographical area, the station still had to be professionally run. I tried my best to overcome my usual nervousness and actually succeeded, for once. Perhaps the knowledge that all the 'proper' DJs had buggered off and left us in the lurch, plus the fact that I was one of so few people on board, made me feel as if my contribution to the programming was actually needed and good enough. From that day on, I never again felt nervous as a DJ.

As it happened, our new schedule was to last no more than a day anyway. As I had often discovered before, on board the *Ross Revenge* you never knew what would happen from one day to the next.

I went to bed after my first full day back on the *Ross*, confident that I had things sorted out with the crew we had on board, and happy that at least there was enough food and plenty of new records, even though there would not be another tender for weeks. As I drifted off to sleep, I couldn't help but feel sorry for the Dutch, who seemed resigned to spending Christmas away from their families (Freddie, still refusing to sail the *Bellatrix* out to us in our hour of need unless we paid him a huge sum of cash in advance). But early the next morning, I woke to the most unexpected sound of the tender bell, and by the time I got up, the *Bellatrix* was tying up off our stern. I was astounded by the sudden appearance of the *Bellatrix* – even more so astounded when I heard Freddie say that he had come out to collect the three Dutch and bring them home as 'an act of kindness'. This from the man who only before I had left land had told me he wouldn't sail unless we paid him!

Speaking to the *Bellatrix*'s skipper, Willie, I got a more interesting view of the situation – apparently news of the major English crew change on Caroline had filtered through to the families of the Dutch DJs in Holland, who then put pressure on Freddie, telling him that, if the English could get their people off the ship, then he could do like-wise – or be exposed in the newspapers as a heartless wretch.

It was sad to say goodbye to the Dutch crew, not knowing when they would be able to return to us, and if we would have a Dutch station at all in the foreseeable future. Erwin, who had been my guide to the ship in my first days on board, was looking disconsolate. As I shook hands with him and wished him well, I told him I was certain that he and I would stand together of the deck of the *Ross Revenge* again in the future. Wim De Walk was the last to leave, and he paused before going, looking me in the eyes. I could see that he too was sad about the Dutch departure from the ship – it was the end of Monique, the end of our cross-cultural community.

'Goodbye Steve,' he said, solemnly shaking hands with me. 'I hope we can be back on board the *Ross* to bring Monique on the air some day in the future.'

'Goodbye Wim,' I said. 'I hope so too.'

As the *Bellatrix* pulled away, and slowly turned to head back to-wards France, Mike Watts and I stood side by side on the back deck, glumly watching our friends departing. Now our battered radio ship had a crew of just four – Mike Watts, John Bibby, Chris and me. There would be just two people to run Caroline, and Chris and I would be doing a six-hour shift each. Just two presenters, an engineer, and a cook, in a ship with fifty-six rooms . . .

I would have liked to put Mike Watts on air, as he had been on during the autumn, but Kevin Turner had expressly forbidden it, so it was down to just Chris and me. It was 'All Irish Radio' as someone later christened it. Thus started a very strange period aboard the *Ross Revenge*: weeks of total solitude. Whenever I was off the air, Chris was on, Mike worked nights doing engineering work and slept during the day, and John only got up in the afternoons. When we were broadcast-ing, it was possible to walk around the ship, and, as long as you did not go into the studio, without meeting a living soul. It was amazing – all those rooms and corridors, usually buzzing with life and activity, all empty and echoing. Only dinner was a sociable activity, and even then, four people spaced around the long messroom table instead of twelve just didn't feel right.

Chris, who had been on the bridge when the giant tower had fallen, described to Mike and myself how it had seemed to almost 'walk sideways across the deck' before slowly – and noisily – collapsing over the starboard side, raining down debris all over the ship. The mast had hung upside down over the side for several hours, attached by several stays, threatening to capsize the ship. For hours, it had smashed against the hull of the ship underwater before finally the last stays parted and it sank into the stormy waters of the Falls Head shortly after dawn.

I had brought out with me a tape which had been passed on to me by a Caroline Movement member, who had happened to be recording Caroline through the night and had captured the last hour of broadcasting from the big tower. We listened to it together one evening, hearing the final link by Pat Brooks, describing how rough it was in the studio as things could be heard banging and crashing in the background.

'This is ridiculous,' Pat had announced as he started what turned out to be the final record broadcast – 'Satellite' by the Hooters. The point of the song that had been reached when the signal cut off contained lyrics that were eerily appropriate as the last words transmitted by a tower that was about to come crashing down into the sea:

> If you fall, well that's OK,
> You love the ones that you betray,
> So jump in the water and learn to swim,
> God's going to wash away all your sins.
> And when at last you see the light,
> God's going to buy you a sat–

In spite of the promise of the lyrics, there was no satellite for us, just a temporary aerial that kept breaking down, and there was hardly a day when we managed to complete an uninterrupted twelve hours on air. The most common problem occurred when the feed-through insulator (i.e. the laundry basket) got wet. Current would arc through it, causing the signal to drop out, and the basket would catch fire. We urgently needed a good insulator but unfortunately six-foot-high moulded ceramic feed-through insulators don't come cheap – or easy – so it looked as though we would have to make do. The atrocious audio quality of our signal on land was reflected in the studio too, where the speakers relayed broadcast signal rather than studio sound.

It wasn't all bad, though – the ship was quiet and peaceful most days, and it was nice to do daytime programming, knowing that the listeners who were still with us were the dedicated followers. And there was plenty of work to be done – like helping Mike to rebuild the newsroom and gathering up and disposing of the debris from the old tower – so I didn't get bored!

And of course, it was my first time on board as a programme controller. I had to spend a couple of hours a day typing out the following day's programme lists, as well as monitoring and adjusting the stations output in terms of style and content at all times. Sunday nights were my busiest – listening to the new UK top 40 on BBC Radio 1, recording any new entries off air if we didn't have them on vinyl, re-jigging our 'A', 'B' and 'C' current-music rotations to take account of the new charts, and deciding which of the new songs being released in the following week would be worthy of inclusion in our 'C' or 'C+' categories (the slow and fast new music rotations). There were quite a few good songs in the charts for December: tracks played on our current rotation included Belinda Carlisle ('Heaven Is A Place On Earth'), Cher ('I Found Someone'), Tiffany ('I Think We're Alone Now') and Heart ('There's the Girl').

Mike rebuilt the newsroom completely, with the teletext TV and computer sealed into a wall unit which he had built himself. So news services were started again, and I had my old job back as well as my new ones.

Gradually the days slipped by, and we began to realise that Christmas might come and go without us seeing a tender. We were now into the darkest days of the year, when the atmospheric conditions after dusk made our signal unlistenable after dark even in Kent. Gradually our mood dipped, as rumours filtered through via our CB contact that

Caroline's finances were exhausted, and that there would be no money to rebuild the radio station, and no new staff.

One particularly bad day, there was a small fault in the 558 transmitter which went unnoticed for hours, and which reduced our coverage area to just a few square miles or so (all water – the nearest land was eighteen miles away) but which wasn't apparent on board. After a long, hard day, when all four of us had worked ourselves to exhaustion doing engineering as well as airtime duties, our CB contact asked us if we were on the air or not, because he couldn't hear us. There we were, happily on air, and a man standing on the beach in Essex couldn't even tell if we were on air or not.

It was two days before Christmas, and we were in a deep state of depression. We talked about things over dinner, and all the worst scenarios were discussed. It seemed obvious that Ronan had no money left, there would be no new towers, and Caroline would eventually run out of fuel. Even our current pitifully low power service would then go off the air. We eventually surmised that Ronan had probably already decided to close Caroline until he could secure major new backing, and that he was letting us have Christmas on the air before disappointing both us and the listeners.

We went to bed at about 11 PM that night, and for the first time ever the ship was left with no one on board awake and on watch. Mike was usually up all night, but that night even he felt that it just wasn't worth it. The ship took care of itself that night, riding the waves with creaks and groans, rolling and turning on the high seas while its four occupants rolled and tossed in an uneasy sleep, deep in her belly. The Falls Head was deserted save for the *Ross Revenge*, which was brightly lit, throbbing with power from its massive generators, home to a crew and the remains of a radio station but, in truth, little more than a ghost ship.

8

ALL ABOUT EVE

DECEMBER 1987–FEBRUARY 1988

The clanging of the tender bell woke me from a troubled sleep. The excited shouts and the scurrying of feet along the cabin corridor outside my door confirmed it – we had a supply boat at long last. I looked at my watch – it was 4 AM on the morning of Christmas Eve. Perhaps we would have a good Christmas after all. It was so cold in my cabin that I put on two jumpers, thick trousers, and a couple of pairs of socks. A blast of icy air greeted me as I went outside, and the people huddled together on the approaching fishing boat looked frozen stiff too. Dave the Fish nudged his craft alongside the *Ross* and Mike Watts took charge, bellowing at us all to tie up this, that or the other, or to get out of his way until everything was done. I was pleased to see three new faces on the tender along with Dave.

The boat had brought us more food and Christmas treats, as well as another huge crate full of engineering supplies and parts for the aerial for Mike. The three newcomers were there to boost our crew complement over Christmas and help with the forthcoming major engineering works, though only one of them was an accomplished DJ. After almost an hour of heavy unloading in the freezing cold, Dave departed and we staggered into the messroom for a cup of hot tea and a chat, to find out what the latest gossip was on land. One of the three newcomers, a friendly-looking guy in his mid-twenties with an almost skinhead haircut, introduced himself as Coconut and said that he had a letter for me from Kevin Turner. I scanned it eagerly. Kevin wrote that things were still progressing on land and that, although money was now tight, there would certainly be enough to pay for a major tender after Christmas, which would bring with it five or six new staff, new mast sections, plenty of copper aerial wire and three engineers – basically everything we would need to build a new high-power mast and aerial system and get Caroline back on the air with a signal covering the whole of England again. Ronan had also arranged for a tug to come to inspect and fix our anchor chain soon after Christmas.

After that excellent news, he went on to thank me for my efforts in keeping the station going with so few staff, and to tell me that of the newcomers, only Coconut, who had worked for the Israeli pirate The Voice Of Peace, should be allowed on air. The second of the three, Eve, was sent to us as a cook, the idea being that John Bibby could either come home or stay on to assist us with mast-building and so on. The other newcomer was Steve Masters, a very young looking eighteen-year-old from Kent, who had ambitions to be a DJ – but who, Kevin said, should be used as a general hand only. Apparently, under normal circumstances he would have been refused work with us because of his age, but in our current position we had to take him. The letter concluded by wishing us a happy Christmas and saying that the big tender should arrive soon after New Year's day. The boost to our morale was tremendous and all the dark thoughts of the night before were instantly forgotten. With a crew of seven, the *Ross Revenge* now seemed to be getting back to normal.

It was a much brighter sounding Caroline that took to the airwaves that morning at 6 AM, and, with the erection of a tree and some decorations in the messroom and the addition of some Christmas songs to the playlists, the whole ship took on a festive air. The newcomers were shown to empty cabins and provided with blankets and other comforts, and were told that they would not be expected to work until the following day, so that they could have a whole day to recover from their tender. I still well remembered the shock of Kevin throwing me in at the deep end within hours of my first arrival on board, and was determined that new crew arriving to find me as deputy programme controller would have a more relaxed introduction, no matter how short-staffed we were.

The day fairly flew by, and before I knew it, it was late afternoon and the sky was darkening. The Olau Line ferry came even closer than usual that afternoon, slowing down as it passed, so that its crew could come out on deck and wave to us. The ferry's captain that day, Captain Ferley, was one of the friendliest on the ferry line, and took his wife and little child out on deck to wave and shout greetings to us. He asked us to play a song on Caroline for his wife, since she usually lived many hundreds of miles away and could not hear us, but this time was with him for Christmas. We were happy to oblige, and played her Ferley's favourite song, 'Captain of Her Heart' by Double!

By dinnertime, our new crew were all up and about and we had a nice lively meal, the messroom full of the sounds of conversation and laughter once more. Over dinner we discussed plans for the Christmas Day programming, which I wanted to be special. Against Kevin's wishes, I wanted Mike Watts to do a programme on Christmas Day: he worked very hard at his engineering duties, and it seemed to me that he should be allowed to have some airtime if he wanted it. I also felt that Mike would considerably enhance the feel of our Christmas line-up by bringing stability and continuity to the station. I was very conscious of the fact that a lot of loyal Caroline listeners would be tuned in over Christmas and felt that Mike's voice on the air on Christmas Day would reassure them that not everybody had deserted us after the mast collapse, and that things were going on in the background to restore the station to its former glory.

Anxious to have the station broadcasting for more than twelve hours on Christmas Day, I also gave in to concerted pleading from John Bibby, who had always wanted to be a DJ, and granted him a show late at night on Christmas night – when reception would be so poor that possibly no one would hear it anyway. Coconut, of course, would be on daytime programmes, but that still left me with the problem of what to do with Steve Masters. Kevin Turner had recruited 'Little Steve' (as we came to call him), telling him that we would 'very probably' be able to use him as a DJ, but then telling me by letter that

117

he was 'not to be allowed anywhere near the studio'. Little Steve was really upset when I told him that he couldn't go on air and could only be a general helper. I felt very sorry for him as he had dropped out of college – incurring the wrath of his family – on the basis of Kevin's offer. He followed me everywhere for the whole of Christmas Eve, and eventually cornered me when I was stuck in the galley doing the washing up.

'Look, I'm going to be really pissed off if I have to spend a whole stint out here doing nothing. Besides, it's simply not fair – Kevin promised me that I could go on air, and now you're telling me that he told you different.'

I shifted uncomfortably on my feet, trying to sound sympathetic, but knowing there was little I could do. I was already going against Kevin's wishes by having Mike Watts on air.

'Look,' he said, coming right up to me and looking me straight in the eyes, 'please give me a programme. Just once, if you like. Try me out to see if I'm any good, and if you don't like me, then you can turf me off the ship and I won't mind, but at least give me that chance.'

I got the letter from Kevin out of my pocket, and looked at it again, the phrase 'not to be allowed anywhere near the studio' screaming out at me from the page.

Little Steve was standing there in front of me, his keen face begging me not to disappoint him. Caroline was his dream too – and who was I to deny him? I remembered some advice that Peter Phillips had given me a few months before. He had said that instructions from land could only ever be guidelines, because only the people actually out on the ship were on the spot, and able to make the real decisions. They had to live with the consequences, and they took the responsibility. I took a deep breath, and made a decision that I knew would cause trouble for me when I next met Kevin, but which I knew in my heart was the right one to make.

'All right, I'll let you do one programme, only one, mark you – late at night tomorrow for two hours – and I'll judge you from that.'

Little Steve let out a whoop of joy and went bounding around the galley, positively beaming with delight. If he fouled up, then at least he would have had his chance, and if he showed promise, I had an extra DJ. Most of all, though, I had stopped one very young and sensitive crew member from having a miserable Christmas.

When I awoke on Christmas morning, the ship was magically still. I was up and dressed by 5 AM, waking Chris with a coffee and pulling his records for him, so that he could slide gently into the first programme of the day. I brought Chris another cup of coffee in the studio just before 6 AM, then wandered out into the record library, to pull the classic tracks for my own programme. In the library, I could listen to Caroline through the speakers, and I heard Chris open up at 6 AM with our theme tune, 'Caroline' by the Fortunes. This was followed, as per the format, by a sixties oldie, then an 'A' list record (a current 'hot' hit). The 'A' was Madonna's 'The Look Of Love', a beautiful, slow and very atmospheric love song, quite unlike her usual frenzied pantings. It drifted out around the ship and, followed by a classic sixties Christmas song, made the *Ross Revenge* feel like some fairy-tale castle in the middle of a snowy wilderness.

There was no snow, of course, but, as dawn broke over the Falls Head, we still had cause for wonder and excitement. As far as the eye could see, the North Sea stretched around us, calm as a millpond. Looking over the side of the ship, you could see your own perfect reflection staring back at you. Unlike on any other day of the year, not a single ship could be seen as far as the horizon – and there we were, eighteen miles offshore, rock-steady in the middle of this calmness, not a breath of wind touching the ship. And this was the middle of winter! It was as if, for Christmas Day, nature had declared a truce and agreed to leave us in peace after all our troubles. And for the first time in weeks, our temporary aerial and transmission system worked faultlessly throughout the whole day and into the night, with not an arc or a crackle.

Mid-morning, I came on the air, following Chris, and did a most enjoyable three-hour programme. By this time, everyone was up and about, and Eve, our new cook, was doing the rounds of the ship offering everyone hot mince pies and tea. John Bibby had decorated the studio, and Mike was busy making stuffing for the turkey, while

Coconut was handing out mini Christmas presents that the Knights from Thanet had sent out to everyone on the ship. There was tinsel and holly everywhere, lots of festive activity going on all around the ship, and a complete absence of the commercialism which so destroys the season on land. It was like heaven.

I really enjoyed that programme and, in the last hour, I made a special dedication to the aardvarks and dedicated followers of Caroline who were listening in. I made a short speech thanking the listeners for their support through a difficult year, and promising that in the new year we would manage, somehow, to rebuild the shattered ship and broadcast to the whole of the UK once more. For Caroline listeners everywhere, I played the song 'Don't Give Up', by Peter Gabriel and Kate Bush, which expressed exactly how we felt.

Mike Watts followed me, and hearing his rich cultured tones and unpretentious links between the music, I felt very glad that we had him on board as part of our Christmas team. My speech would doubtless have allayed some of our supporters' fears, but the programme from Mike Watts would reinforce the feeling that the 'Caroline family' was still together, no matter how many people had left. After Mike came Coconut, doing his first ever programme on Caroline, and I was reasonably pleased with the way he sounded. He certainly knew how to handle the equipment, and was quite competent at linking between records, even if our format did restrict him slightly in terms of style.

As it was Eve's first working day aboard the vessel, Mike stepped in to help with the Christmas dinner. He displayed considerable culinary flair, delivering one of the most sumptuous Christmas feasts I have ever had. Was there *anything* this man wasn't good at?

After dinner, there were more pies and other goodies, and by about 8 PM we were all almost inert in the messroom, stuffed to the gills, and very happy. John Bibby was now on the air, sounding very amateurish, and I winced at times listening to him – but thankfully it was now after dark, and our signal coverage area would have shrunk to almost nothing.

By the time I felt lively enough to do the washing up, Little Steve Masters was just taking to the air for his trial programme. I listened with interest through the speaker in the galley. Despite a lot of minor failings, I couldn't help but feel that I detected in him the glimmerings of some real talent and style. I mentioned this to Mike, who listened and agreed with me. Yes, he sounded poor at the moment, but with some encouragement, and a lot of practice, he had the makings of a good presenter.

Little Steve, of course, was thrilled to bits when I told him as much after his programme, and I said that, while we were still on low power, he could continue to do shifts, and I would continue to review his progress. That conversation over, I went downstairs to bed, not at all unhappy at the outcome of the day's events.

New Year's Eve was another day in which Caroline programming traditionally departed from the norm – usually there was a Top 100 countdown of the year leading up to midnight, with a 'party'-style programme. I consulted with Mike, who agreed that we could broadcast throughout the night on 31 December, and he said he would increase the power fractionally so that our signal might just reach land for that evening's programmes. The power increase could only be temporary, though – more than a couple of days on even a slightly higher power, and our laundry-basket insulator would burn itself out. In order that the countdown would be heard by the widest possible audience, I moved it from its traditional midnight slot to mid-afternoon, when our coverage area included the whole of Kent and parts of Essex.

For the Top 100, I listed all the chart records of 1987 currently rotating in our 'Z' list (very recent oldies) and produced a form on which each person on the ship could register votes against each song. This way, the Top 100 would represent broader tastes than just my own, without aping the BBC or ILR Top 100s. The song which was voted Number 1 of the year by the Caroline crew was 'What Have I Done to Deserve This' by the Pet Shop Boys and Dusty Springfield, while one of my own favourites of the year, 'Alone' by Heart, came in the top three. The New Year's Eve's programmes went very well, and the evening show was quite festive – due perhaps to Eve's spiking of my Coke with something a little more potent. I had started over the previous few days to flirt with Eve and the spiked drink removed many of my inhibitions. The rest of the crew watched in fits of laughter that evening, as my amorous pursuit of her became more and more heated – and comical.

At midnight, Mike sounded the ship's horn across the empty seas, and we called up the coastguard on the ship-to-shore radio to wish them a happy New Year.

Nineteen-eighty-eight obviously intended to start with a bang, as by nightfall on its first day we were in the grips of north-westerly gales, and the ship was rolling savagely from side to side. From that day onwards, we had strong north or north-westerly winds, with the sea usually rough. The *Ross Revenge*, still wrongly ballasted for the missing tower, rolled and twisted like a rodeo horse trying to shake off its human inhabitants. Sometimes the seas got so rough that we were afraid the anchor chain would snap. On those occasions, Mike started ancillary equipment in the engine room to ensure that, if the worst happened, we would be ready to start our main engine without delay, and sail away from danger. Most of the time, though, it was more uncomfortable than dangerous, and inconvenient in-so-much as the salt from the waves breaking over the main deck ensured that the plastic laundry basket rapidly began to disintegrate, and we were more often off the air than on.

Routine chores such as getting fresh bread out of the freezers (which were located in the forepeak at the front of the ship) became a challenge of skill and speed – timing your dash along the deck between rolls and waves, so that you were neither hurled off your feet nor drenched up to the knees. And the records, which had always stayed on the shelves no matter how bad the weather, now hurled themselves onto the floor with grim determination. Sometimes we had to post someone in the library solely to push them back as they marched towards the edge of the shelves, and even then we sometimes ended up with most of the library on the floor.

Mike had his hands full at this stage, constantly having to switch us off and make minor repairs whenever the laundry-basket insulator broke down, which was usually twice a day. The constant battering by waves breaking over the deck, and more salt spray, took its toll and, one day while Little Steve was on the air, the signal disappeared. We rushed to the window to see the entire basket engulfed in flames, with molten plastic dripping all over the wooden deck. Had it not been for the constant waves, it would doubtless have set the deck on fire. Even so, by the time Mike was able to get to the transmitter room and switch it off, the basket was a charred mass of blackened plastic.

Now we were off the air permanently until we could replace the basket. Mike had some ideas for a new insulator fashioned out of a plastic rainwater barrel, but until the weather died down it would be impossible for him to work out on deck to install it. It quickly became boring without Caroline on the air, and by the second day most of the crew were prowling around looking for mischief. Playing around in the deserted 558 studio, I made an interesting discovery. By pressing certain buttons on the mixer, I could pipe the output of the studio to the speakers around the ship, even though the station was off the air. As these speakers had always been exclusively off-air monitors, a plan began to form in my mind. I called Chris and Coconut up to the studio, the others all being in bed, and told them what I was plotting. Steve Masters had been in bed almost constantly since we went off the air, and was refusing to get up and help out with routine chores. But if he thought we were back on the air . . .

We set it up so that Coconut was 'on air' in the 558 studio. Chris and I went downstairs to wake Little Steve, telling him we were back on the air, and that he had to be on air soon. He didn't believe us, so we turned on the speaker in his cabin, and he heard what sounded like the station operating as normal – and shot out of bed. A similar stunt was then played on Mike Watts, the idea being that Chicago had dropped in by helicopter while he was asleep and put us back on the air. Mike saw through it at once, and called our bluff. He pointed out that while all this had been going on, we had failed to notice that the weather had improved slightly – enough to get on with the work of building a new insulator.

Mike worked into the night and on a number of occasions we were required out on deck, in relays, to hand him tools and help him. The station was back on the air the following day. Although the weather quickly worsened again, Mike's new insulator substitute proved more durable than its predecessor, and we stayed on with fewer breaks.

Gradually the days passed, in a flurry of white horses and stormy sunsets, and we soon found ourselves in mid-January, still without a tender or new masts. We also needed a tug to repair our anchor-chain, which had a rapidly weakening link. True, Mike had tweaked the broadcast system to make it more reliable, but it was still basically a 'coathanger' aerial, capable of reaching only a few miles inland. As far as listeners beyond of Kent and Essex were concerned, we had vanished in November and never returned.

After what seemed like an endless wait, but was in reality only a couple of weeks, the *Bellatrix* eventually arrived out in mid-January with a huge amount of engineering supplies, and lots of people to do the work, including Peter Philips, Chicago and Ernie. They also brought a large extendible metal tower, which took considerable effort to bring across to the *Ross*.

We quickly realised that we had only got one of the two one-hundred-foot towers that would be necessary to set up a proper 'T' aerial system. Chicago told us that we had as much as Ronan had been able to buy with the money he had left and that it was up to us to build another mast ourselves, get Caroline back on high power, and get the Dutch on the air again, one way or another. Apparently Ernie had an idea which involved using disused materials from the ship's days as a trawler to fashion a new hundred-foot front mast; the collapsible tower would reach the same height, sprouting from the back deck. The *Bellatrix* would be staying with us as long as was necessary to get the job done, so that we would have extra hands, and the use of its crane.

During a break for tea, Peter Phillips filled us in on the rest of the news from land. He said Ronan had drawn up an elaborate three-stage plan for our recovery. After the new 'T' system had been built, we would take delivery of two of the new fibreglass 'wonder-masts' which were meant to transmit very powerful signals by themselves with no aerial array. He had gone ahead and bought these against the advice of both Mike Watts and Chicago, and they were being shipped across from Canada as we spoke. Then – and this was probably pure fantasy

– there would be a new four-hundred-foot mast, a hundred feet taller than the one we had lost, with the top hundred and fifty feet made of fibreglass to reduce weight. We would build the bottom half, and the top half would be flown out complete by helicopter, and carefully lowered into position. The idea of using a helicopter to fly a mast out to a radio ship had first been mooted by Ronan in the seventies with the *Mi Amigo*. It had never happened then, and would probably never happen now. Chicago, Watts and Phillips were under no illusions – unless we managed to build a new twin-tower 'T' aerial system with what we had on board now, there would probably be nothing at all in the future. And if we did build a good 'T', and get Caroline back on the air properly, the other plans would disappear anyway, as no one would want to interrupt a newly recovered station for yet more engineering works.

We quickly worked out an action plan that involved every single person on both the *Ross* and the *Bellatrix* crew working on the project. We were split into small groups, supervised by the people who really knew what they were doing: Chicago, Mike Watts, and Ernie. We would work from dawn through to nightfall and beyond, breaking only for meals, as we could not afford to waste the sudden spell of calm weather.

Chicago set his crew to work on the back deck of the *Ross*, where they were positioning and welding down huge metal plates, which would form a stable and secure base for the new extendible mast. New staying points had to be made and welded to the deck, and old ones refurbished if they were in a suitable position.

Peter Phillips and Mike were working on the front deck with their helpers, inspecting the ship's original front mast, which was at least fifty feet too short for what they now needed it to do. I ended up with Ernie, who was cutting down sections of disused piping to weld to the front mast to increase its height. Last thing on the first day, the entire crew congregated amidships to lower down the temporary aerial, which was now in the way of Peter Phillips's work on the front mast. With that down, and lying forlornly curled up on the deck, we could not broadcast, even on low power. Everything depended on us getting two complete masts built, erected, stayed and insulated, and hoisting up an aerial, before the next spell of bad weather came. According to the BBC, we had four days before the winds would get up again.

The ship was full of the sounds of grinding, cutting, hammering, dragging and welding. Ernie found a long stretch of piping which had been used in the ship's days as a trawler to carry cod-liver oil to large tanks in the engine room. The pipe was cut down from the ceiling and fell with a tremendous crash. The stench of ten-year-old cod-liver oil filled the ship, driving everyone retching out on deck. The cod-liver oil came out of the pipe in a sticky, almost solid mess, and within days had been trampled throughout the ship. We now had to cut a hole in the side of the ship to get the pipe out on deck: it was far too long to fit through a doorway. Once this had been done, even the inside of the ship was strafed by the bitterly cold winds which swept down from the north across the Falls Head – though at least they helped clear out the smell a bit.

The four days of calm weather passed in a blur of hard physical work, and it quickly became apparent that the task was far bigger than we had imagined. The extendible tower was fixed in place on the back deck, but not extended or stayed, and the front mast was still lying in pieces on the main deck when the north-westerly gales resumed and the *Bellatrix* had to leave us, taking Mike Watts, Chris and John Bibby with it.

The weather died down after a few days, and it became calm enough for us all to work outside on deck again. The mast on the back deck was bolted and welded down, but Peter didn't want to extend it to its full height until we had extra metalwork from land. So we concentrated on assembling the new front mast, which was being built horizontally along the deck, to be hauled up into position later. Sections of pipe had to be ground smooth, welded and checked, cross members had to be added and stays attached, and the whole thing had to be primed and painted.

It was sunset on the last day of January as the incredible structure, part cod-liver-oil pipe, part trawler mast, part scaffold pole, was slowly winched upright. Halfway up, it started to sag and bend horribly in the

126

middle, and we were all afraid that it would snap, but it made it and was soon lashed into position, standing proud and tall at almost a hundred foot, the tallest thing on the ship since the previous November. By this time it was dark, but Peter decided that all the stays should be attached and tightened that night, in effect completing that phase of the work and making the mast completely secure.

As we finished this work, lights were seen coming towards us in the darkness, and Dave the Fish was soon alongside in his little fishing boat, having brought us the extra stays and metalwork needed to complete the back mast, as well as more copper aerial wire. Also with the tender came some unexpected, and sobering, news – the Laser ship, *Communicator*, despite efforts to raise finance, rebuild its masts and get back on the air, had finally run out of money. There had been a number of power struggles and potential takeovers both on and off the ship, and the ship's engineer, fed up with the whole situation, had sailed her into Harwich and surrendered to the authorities, in a carbon copy of what had happened to Laser 558 in 1985. The *Communicator* had been impounded, and tied up by the authorities well inland on the river Stour, so we were now the only surviving radio ship on the high seas. Unless we got our act together and returned to the air soon, what had happened to them could easily happen to us.

That night we all went to bed in reasonably high spirits, but by dawn the following morning we were in the grip of one of the most violent storms we had encountered throughout that winter. The winds swung round to the north and rose steadily to storm force 10 and beyond. Massive swollen waves, built up over thousands of miles of empty sea, smashed over our bow, drenching the ship and making the entire structure of the vessel shake.

Shortly after dawn, the *Ross* turned to take the waves sideways, and started rolling violently from side to side, so that I was literally thrown from one side of the ship to another. It was lucky indeed that Peter Phillips had insisted on fully securing the stays on our new mast the night before. Shortly after midday, I ventured into the galley, intending to make myself a cup of coffee. Eve had left a large, catering size tub of mayonnaise on the work surface the night before, and this had fallen on to the floor and split. When a particularly large wave rammed the ship over on one side, I went flailing and landed, cup in hand, in the middle of the pool of mayonnaise. The cup shattered under me, and blood began to mix with the creamy mess. I struggled to get up, but my feet kept slipping from under me, the rolling of the ship constantly knocking me off balance.

Bang! I was slammed into the wall by a lurch of the ship, then, before I could recover, I went spinning across the slimy floor, to crash into some pipes sticking out of the far wall. Back and forth I went, getting ever more bruised and bloody. The ship kept rolling, the floor kept spinning, and I realised that unless I got up soon, I would be battered beyond belief. Salvation came in the shape of Chicago, who spotted me as he was carefully making his way along the main corridor, tightly gripping the handrail. He chuckled at the sight of me, but quickly lent a hand to extricate me from my sticky mess. Luckily, my plight was not as bad as it had seemed at first; just a cut hand and a lot of bruises.

The storm died down as quickly as it had blown up, and work commenced on welding extra metal sections into the new back tower, preparing the stays and attaching the crosstrees. The crosstrees (large metal segments used for spreading the load of the stays) had been ordered by Chicago, but the ones we had been sent were far smaller and thinner than we had requested. As the first of them was hoisted into position, Chicago was heard to comment: 'They're not cross trees – more like pissed-off saplings.'

When it became obvious that the work would take us several days to complete, Chicago took a couple of hours off to re-erect the original temporary short aerial, this time between the funnel and a point two-thirds up the new front tower. This would allow us to go back on the air, still on very low power: with all the work now concentrated on the back, it was safe to have the front one live. Although it would only be the same sort of short-range low power transmission as we had had over Christmas, at least it would put us on the air for the time being. We had now been 'off' for almost three weeks, far longer than when the tower itself had fallen down in November.

So Caroline limped back into life again, once more covering the coastal towns of Kent and Essex with a weak and unreliable signal. At least we were on, though, and we had something to do on the days when it was too rough to work.

Gradually, over the next week or so, the back mast came together, finally rising ninety feet into the air, nearly matching the height of the front one. Now all that remained was for Chicago to make up the giant aerial array that would go between the two masts, dropping down in the centre, like the 'T' it was named after, to our feed-through point into the transmitter room. Our aerial was to be made of four thick copper wires, which ran slightly apart from each other, sausage-like, the length and height of the array. Chicago set up shop on the main deck, cutting and twisting the wire, making up the spacers needed to keep the wires from touching, and attaching the whole thing to the ropes and pulleys that we would use to haul it a hundred feet up into the air.

The morning of 12 February dawned fine and clear, and we closed down our low-powered transmissions. Within minutes, a work-team was pulling down the Mark 2 temporary aerial array and clearing it out of the way. Before we could hoist up Chicago's new system, Peter Phillips had to do some more work at the top of the front mast, adjusting the staying points and insulators. Unlike our old tower, which he used to climb fairly easily, this was a smooth thin pipe, so to get to the top he had to sit in a little cradle and be winched up on a pulley system. Peter spent several hours at the top of the mast; when he came down, we were ready to begin. Slowly but surely, we began the work of hoisting the new aerial up into the sky. When it got dark, we tied it off and retired inside for the night.

The following morning, everyone was up and outside at first light. We knew that by the end of the day we should be on the air again on high power. We couldn't wait. I ended up working with Chicago that morning on top of the Monkey Island. It was a bitterly cold day and up there on top of the ship the wind cut straight through you. Before long I was frozen stiff, and numb with cold, but I continued working for as long as Chicago needed me, as did the others below. Caroline was

129

close to being reborn, and we would do anything, no matter how uncomfortable, to hasten the process.

Finally the aerial was hoisted fully into position, attached to the insulators at either end, and to the plastic feed-through insulator at deck level. We now had two hundred-foot masts, with a well-crafted and stylish 'T' aerial hung between them. All we had to do now was wait for Chicago to tune the transmitter to the aerial and declare that we were back on the air.

Dinner came and went, and Chicago stayed locked away downstairs, working on his transmitters. At about 8 PM, he requested us to feed some audio through from the studio, and we did that, playing a couple of records so that he could have a modulated signal to test with. Chicago then disappeared off again and left us alone. Later that night, Chicago strolled casually into the messroom, cup of tea in hand. We knew better than to ask him how he was getting on – Chicago had a wicked sense of humour, and if he detected any anxiety in our queries, would string the whole business out forever. He finished his tea, he got up, and opened the door to leave the messroom.

'I'm off to bed now – goodnight everyone,' he said, ducking to go out the door. He then poked his head back around the door and gave a grin. 'Oh by the way, I don't suppose anyone's interested, but we're on and ready now, so hadn't someone go up to the studio and start programming?'

Peter Phillips was in bed but had told me to commence programmes as necessary. I approached the studio almost reverently, followed by Steve Masters and Coconut. The studio was warm and softly lit, the clock ticking away, and everything ready and waiting for just this moment. I sat down in the studio chair, beginning to realise the importance of what was about to happen. It was 10:53 on the night of 13 February.

I picked out a record from the Loving Awareness Band 'Love You to Know', an old Caroline staple, and gently started it running, listening to the sound of clear, undistorted audio filling the studio. I let the record play out, watching the hands of the clock sweep closer to 11 PM. I fired off 'Caroline' by the Fortunes, and felt the station swell into life around me. The first normal record of the show was all ready on the turntable, waiting for me to start it at the end of our theme song. The Caroline bell jingle, always used as the station ID, was ready for play in the cart machine. As the Fortunes faded away, I pressed the start button of the first record and opened my microphone.

For the best part of three long months, Caroline had been off the air, or barely alive on a low-powered distorted signal. Now, for the first time since that November night back in 1987, we could be heard across the length and breadth of England, France, Belgium and Holland.

'On 558 Kilohertz, this is Radio Caroline.' Ding ding.

There were whoops of joy from the others behind me.

We were back on the air, on high power, and soon people all over the UK would discover that the station which had vanished overnight in November was back in business.

It felt great.

9

THE DRIFTERS

FEBRUARY–APRIL 1988

With Caroline back on full power on 558, the priority was to get income coming in quickly. Chicago put together a simple but efficient aerial array to allow short wave tests to recommence. The backers of the proposed religious station, which would have been on air before Christmas had it not been for the mast disaster, wanted to hear two solid months of reliable testing before parting with any money. We kept the short wave running throughout March, relaying Caroline 558, and hoping that Ronan could work his magic with them. Further expensive engineering supplies would be needed if we were to get a second medium wave frequency running for the Dutch service, and it was hoped that the short wave religion would pay for this.

By the end of March, things were looking hopeful, but we were not to know that an entirely new set of problems was waiting just around the corner. As usual, disaster struck when we were least expecting it.

One Sunday night, I was hard at work in the newsroom, preparing the next week's current rotations from the new top forty, scanning the list of new single releases on teletext to see if there were any we had on vinyl, and working out which of the recordings I had made of Johnny Walker's programme on BBC Radio 1 the previous day could be edited into playable form for our 'C' and 'C+' new-music lists. Peter Philips had taken a break, and I was running the station again, this time on full power, with a potentially large audience, so I was trying to keep the music selection as fresh as possible. A record six weeks had gone by without any tender, so new music was thin on the ground.

Outside the news-room porthole, the Falls Head was an expanse of flat calm sea, broken only by the regular flashing of the buoy some three-quarters of a mile distant. The sea around us seemed as innocent and inviting as it had the day we had moved to the Falls Head the previous summer.

Downstairs, Mike Watts was preparing to go on air with an overnight programme, and Little Steve was busy in the galley, having promised to make doughnuts out of ingredients he had picked up from the food stores. The generators were humming away content-edly, the station was running smoothly, and all was well with the world. I worked well into the night before finally completing what I decided was an acceptable current playlist for the new week. When supplies of music were up to date, the job was usually finished by about 10 or 11 PM, but we had had no records for almost eight weeks, and I was rely-ing heavily on material recorded from Radio 1, the BBC TV *Wogan* chatshow (which often had a band or artist on performing their new single), the ITV chart show and other sources. This all had to be trans-ferred off cassette, edited (to remove voiceovers or clapping) and carted up for airplay and it was almost 2 AM before I was finished.

Among the new material introduced that night was 'Beds Are Burning' by Midnight Oil and 'Fast Car' by Tracy Chapman, two tracks which were not due for release for a couple of weeks yet, but which I had included in our C list because I felt they were very good, and be-cause they would help keep us sounding fresh. I had recorded both from Johnny Walker's programme on Radio 1 the day before. Thank-fully he had played them in their entirety, without any voiceover or an-noying jingles, so we had them complete. Tracy Chapman's 'Fast Car' was particularly exciting: Johnny had received an exclusive advance copy on tape, Tracy Chapman was unknown at this time, and he was the very first person to play her in the UK. Within hours of that sin-gle play on the BBC, with Johnny's tape the only copy of the song, she would be getting regular airplay in a fast rotation on Caroline . . .

I came up from the studio and wandered back into the record library, drained after several hours of editing, typing and thinking, and sat on the comfortable sofa seat, listening to the station through the wall speaker to hear what the new list sounded like. Little Steve came up with a plate of what could be only very loosely described as doughnuts. They were nice on the outside, but undercooked inside, and with a very peculiar tang. He explained that he had used too much of something or other in the mix, and half of the doughnuts had exploded in the oven. Nevertheless, as we had long since run out of everything other than basic foodstuffs, they were eaten anyway. Little Steve and I got to talking, and decided that what we were really missing on the *Ross Revenge* was chocolate. Like me, he had brought a small supply from land when he came back from shoreleave, but these stashes had long since been exhausted. Other luxuries we could do without, and shortages of such things as tea, milk and meat could be borne stoically, but chocolate – the yearning just never went away.

The only thing we had on board that was remotely chocolate-like was a Dutch substance called Hagel that, if munched by the mouthful, did give one a slight feeling of chocolate. Hagel was actually thousands of miniature chocolate grains, each about half the size of a grain of rice. The Radio Monique DJs used to sprinkle this liberally over their food – even over things like eggs or meat, or buttered bread, and, as our supplies had been organised by the Dutch, there were dozens of packets still piled up in the food stores at the back of this ship.

Talking about chocolate had made our yearning worse, so we decided to experiment with ways of refining Hagel to make proper chocolate, or at least an approximation of it. We settled eventually on melting the Hagel down in a pan, adding sugar and a little milk, then allowing it to set. The result was absolutely disgusting – over-rich, sticky and messy as hell, but, as true chocolate lovers, we scoffed the lot.

While sitting eating the 'chocolate', Little Steve and I chatted away, our conversation eventually coming round to the topic of the authorities, and their views on Radio Caroline. Over the past couple of weeks, we had been visited by a couple of coastguard and British Navy vessels, who had anchored near us for a few hours, watching us and taking pictures. We discussed how the British government was always deeply suspicious of the motives of those who worked for the station, failing to comprehend why we would go to so much trouble and endure such an isolated life just to play music; suspicious that we must be involved in some huge international conspiracy to smuggle drugs or cigarettes. The *Ross Revenge* was frequently photographed from the outside by both official ships and aircraft, but they would dearly love to get a glimpse of the things that its wicked inhabitants got up to out of sight inside the vessel. We laughed at the thought of how disappointed they would be if they planted bugging devices on board the *Ross*, only to find that we were spending the dark hours of the night making illicit doughnuts and chocolate.

Little Steve then made me a surprising offer – he would cover the morning news shift, allowing me to sleep in until midday. Coming from someone who had once had the reputation of being the laziest person on board, this was a real shock, and an indication of how much he had changed over his two stints out at sea. I accepted gratefully, and clambered into my bunk down in Cabin 9 in a state of exhausted contentment.

I slept well, and awoke at about midday, my cabin below the waterline having provided perfect darkness. I put on a dressing gown, and wandered up to the shower room near the studios, determined to start the new week off feeling clean. I opened the porthole in the shower room, stripped off, and luxuriated in the hot water. Glancing out of the porthole, a strange sight snapped me out of my still-sleepy state. The Falls Head buoy was almost directly outside the shower room window – not three quarters of a mile away, where it should have been – but literally less than twenty yards distant.

'Shit!' I exclaimed, grabbing my dressing gown, bursting out from the shower room half naked and making for the stairs up to the bridge at a run, trailing water behind me.

I knew immediately what that sight meant: either the Falls Head buoy had moved more than half a mile away from its proper location, or we had.

Given the clockwork regularity with which all the buoys in the channel were serviced, it was immediately clear to me that we were the ones who had moved – *were* moving. The newsroom was deserted, Little Steve having gone to bed after the 9 AM news, and the Decca Navigator, kept to pinpoint our location at all times, was flashing away in the corner, its screen showing the message 'Drift Alarm'. I looked at the co-ordinates, but already knew from our position relative to the buoy that we had moved just over half a mile to the north-east. Our anchor chain had broken, or the anchor was dragging, and in anything other than the flat, calm weather we were experiencing, this would have caused us serious problems. With no anchor, we would be swept away from the Falls Head. To our north lay vast empty seas, but to the south and west lay land – rocks, and sandbanks, as well as the busy Dover Straits and the Goodwin Sands due south of us. And of course British territorial waters . . . I had to find Mike.

Mike was sitting alone down in the transmitter room. He told me that he had made the same discovery just minutes earlier, and was thinking about how to break it to the others without causing them unnecessary alarm.

We monitored our position during the afternoon, giving the CB contact a message for the office to contact us urgently and to arrange a tug, as we were drifting. We then discussed the situation with the rest of the crew over dinner.

Mike explained to everyone that the *Ross Revenge* was now about a mile and a half away from its normal location, and that the ship seemed to be moving very slowly back and forwards on the tide. Unlike previous occasions when the *Ross Revenge* had lost its anchor, the break had happened in calm conditions, so the ship was staying relatively stable. This seemed to indicate that the break was well down the chain, near the bottom, and that the weight of the chain was countering the tidal currents. This situation would change rapidly if the weather worsened.

Mike then explained that our land team had been alerted, and that they would doubtless organise a tug to fix our chain and re-anchor us – probably within twenty-four hours. In the meantime we would have to maintain a constant watch on the bridge and keep track of our position on the charts. Mike then instructed everyone on the ship's emergency drill, including the donning of lifejackets, and said that the following morning he would give everyone a basic lesson in operating the winches, safety gear and other equipment that might be needed should we get into further difficulties. Meanwhile, he would start the engine-room generators and ancillary equipment, and warm up the main engine, in case we should need to sail under our own power.

By 10 PM that night, all the engine-room equipment apart from the engine itself was running – the main engine would only be started if absolutely necessary, as it guzzled fuel – and everything was ready to cope with any possible emergency. We were double – and triple – shifting now to provide a permanent watch on the bridge and twenty-four hour cover in the engine room, as well as continuing to run the radio station, but Mike had managed to turn the atmosphere into one of a sort of suppressed excitement. Shortly after 11 PM, Chicago called us on his special radio link from Margate, wanting to confirm that the message he had received from our CB man in Essex about us being adrift was true. We assured him that it was and he said that he would try to get in touch with Ronan and get him to organise some help for us. Chicago signed off, and we went about our duties, knowing that at least someone on land was aware of the situation, and working to help us.

The next morning saw us three miles north of the Falls Head, drifting slowly back towards it on the tide. By the time Mike assembled us all at 2 PM for our safety lessons, we were close enough to the buoy to read the inscription on the side.

Mike took us all around the front of the ship, showing us the anchor winches, chain-runs and spare anchor chain, and explaining how it could be used if necessary. Our spare anchor chain was too thin and short for normal use, but it could be used to stop us if we came dangerously close to the coastline. We then descended though the levels of disused rooms below the forepeak, ending up at the very bottom of the front of the ship, in the chain locker. From here, two of us would work to ensure that the spare chain fed smoothly up through the run to the deck above, where others would be able to drop it, if this became necessary. Mike explained to each person what his job would be in the event of crisis, then took us back out into the sunlight, explaining that in all probability we would see a tug arriving soon.

But the tug didn't arrive, that day or the next, and the week dragged on into a sort of hazy unreality: each morning we would be in some new location, every day the ship would move of its own accord as the tides dragged it hither and thither. Sometimes we would be dumped back at the Falls Head, other times we would be many miles away from it. Miraculously, the weather held, so we were never in any real danger. A surveillance helicopter came out to look at us at one stage, but we ignored it: we were not planning to tell the authorities about our problems unless they became serious, as they would only have tied up lifeboat and helicopter crews needlessly to watch over us. Eventually, after what seemed like an eternity, the dawn light showed us the *Bellatrix* sitting at anchor a mile or so away, doubtless waiting for full light before coming to assist us.

I was on the air when the big blue tender made its approach, but it came in on our starboard side, so I had a good view of proceedings from the studio window. As the *Bellatrix* drew closer, I was pleased to see Peter Phillips, Chicago and Ernie, as well as Freddie and Willie – and then surprised to see the familiar face of Ad Roberts – a Dutch DJ who was returning to the *Ross* for the first time since the tower had collapsed!

Ad and some other Dutch were there because the *Bellatrix* crew had brought the final materials to erect the fibreglass 'wonder tower' that Ronan had bought to put the Dutch station back on the air again. They would be staying until the job was done, and a tug was scheduled to arrive sometime over the weekend, to repair our anchor chain and re-establish us at the Falls Head. An English tender would also be arriving soon, with further supplies and fresh staff.

Soon after I finished my programme, I managed to corner Peter, and find out the latest developments concerning the radio station. Our chat left me feeling upset and depressed. Peter was not, in fact, returning to the *Ross Revenge* to stay – he had been offered a job on our rival, the Kent station Invicta Radio, and would be going back to land along with the *Bellatrix* after the work was done and the ship had been re-anchored. He had come back out primarily to help with the erection of the mast, and also to let me know that he was actually leaving the station.

Peter was quite pessimistic about Caroline, and explained that he had been treated badly, and been left unpaid when he returned to shore in February, after the two months of hard mast building, which had got 558 back on full power. He also expressed disappointment at how Caroline had been running during his time on land, saying that he thought I could have coped better with the problems caused by staff and music shortages if I had tried harder. Peter then explained that an English tender would be arriving that night with new staff, but that he would like me to stay on for a while longer. I thought differently, however. If Peter was leaving, I would be on my own running the format, and I should really take a quick break while he was still at the Falls Head with the *Bellatrix* work-crew and then come back soon afterwards, refreshed for what might turn out to be a very long stint.

There was little time for me to brood on what Peter had said though, as the ship was now a hive of activity, with all the new arrivals rushing around doing preparatory work for the installation of the new fibreglass mast system. Peter and Chicago set to work converting a disused room at the rear of the ship to hold tuning and aerial feed equipment, Freddie and Willie were working on the back deck preparing mounting plates for the base of the mast, and Ernie was checking the engines in case we should need to sail the ship before the tug arrived. After helping Chicago, I retired to the newsroom to keep an eye on our current location – and got quite a shock. The extra weight of the *Bellatrix* hanging off the *Ross Revenge* was obviously causing us to drag our chain and drift much faster, as we were now some six miles away from the Falls Head, and moving rapidly northwards. Tracking our course on the sea-chart, I saw that we would soon come to a spot where British waters curved out into our path – meaning that in something less than half an hour, we would be officially within UK jurisdiction.

I rushed downstairs and gave this news to Chicago but, to my surprise, he seemed to be not too worried, being more concerned about the engineering tasks in hand. I told him I would notify him when we came near the limit, and went back upstairs. At about 5 PM, we came to the territorial limit, and passed within it, and I duly notified Chicago and Mike Watts. To my surprise, they said that we should stay on the air, as our course would take us back into international waters in an hour or so, and a sudden closedown would only attract attention to us at a time when we would be most vulnerable. And so, for a while in the early evening of 1 April 1988, Radio Caroline was knowingly broadcasting from within the United Kingdom – a unique occurrence.

Heavy engineering work on the ship continued well after darkness fell, though unlike the work of January and February, the station was able to stay on the air during all the work, as the 819 system would be completely separate from the existing 558 one. After dinner, Ernie and Chicago started the ship's main engines, as we were now twelve miles north of the Falls Head, and still heading north at an amazing rate. The ship rumbled and trembled under our feet, full of unusual sounds and noises. I finished my last watch on the bridge at midnight and went down to bed, determined to get some sleep before the possible tender the next day.

In bed in Cabin 9, I finally had time to think back to my conversation with Peter Phillips, and my mood gradually sank. Peter's comments about the way the ship had been run during March grated on me because, although deep down I knew they were true, I had nonetheless tried to do my best during six very difficult weeks. I felt that he could have given me a little more credit for the fact that circumstances had been, in the main, against me. Knowing that Peter himself was leaving made things worse too. If I was not good enough to deputise in his absence, how could I possibly run the station after he had gone? Who could I rely on as my deputy? The fact that my last day working on board with Peter, who had taught me everything, and whom I greatly admired, was one during which he was displeased with me made me feel even worse.

I was wakened from a troubled sleep by Mike, who told me that it was 4 AM, and the English tender had arrived – Dave the Fish, with his small boat from Ramsgate. I was up and dressed quickly, but before heading for the tender, I went up to my favourite thinking spot at the bow of the ship, and sat on my own for a little while, watching the activity on the decks below, and wondering if it was time for me to follow in the footsteps of the many people who had gradually left over the past year. I wasn't sure; it would need more thought.

Returning to the main deck, I started to climb over the deck rail and across to the tender.

'Steve.' Chicago came rushing up to me. 'I just wanted to say goodbye and wish you a good shore leave.'

I had told no one how I felt, and was surprised when Chicago suddenly reached out and gripped me in a firm handshake, looking me straight in the face. 'I'll be hoping to see you out here again before too long, Steve,' he said, his eyes boring into me, and his handshake seeming to give me some of his strength. 'Enjoy yourself – but you make sure you come back out here soon.'

There was real warmth, and a genuine invitation, in his voice. I didn't know how he had guessed at my mood, but the message to me from Chicago was unmistakable. As far as he was concerned, I belonged on the ship, and was wanted back. I clambered over the *Bellatrix* and down the other side, its scramble-net having been unrolled to make our passage easy. And then I was on the fishing boat, which was casting its lines away and chugging towards the English coast. As always, the *Ross Revenge* was a beautiful sight, all lights and reflections on the moonlit sea, seemingly made even more beautiful by the brightly lit *Bellatrix* beside it.

The trip into Ramsgate on the *FourWinds* was the longest I had ever encountered. I had not had time to check the *Ross*'s position when I had been woken for the tender, but apparently it was almost seventeen miles away from the Falls Head. As a result, the trip to shore was twice as long as usual.

Eventually we arrived in Ramsgate, where it was grey and drizzly. Just outside the harbour, the fishing boat halted, having been denied the usual entry clearance by Ramsgate Harbour Control. The wait made us suspicious, but when we were eventually granted permission to dock, the harbour seemed deserted and there was no-one in authority around. We dragged our bags and belongings up the metal ladders to the quayside, and along to Dave the Fish's van, which was parked nearby. I said my goodbyes and parted from the others, as I had a message to bring to Chicago's wife, Carol, in Margate, and I intended to get a local bus from the town centre, while the others were getting a lift to the station. I walked off along the footpath out of the harbour, waving at the others as they passed. I was carrying only one small bag: I usually left more belongings on the *Ross* than I took on land. The others had all had huge rucksacks, or, in the case of Little Steve, suitcases.

As I came to the end of the road leading from the docks, an unnerving sight met me. The van had been stopped at a police roadblock, and Dave and the others were standing by it, being questioned by officers, while police went through the contents of the luggage. Another police car was parked at the entrance to the other quayside that we might have docked at – obviously they had been waiting for us, and the delay in allowing us to enter the harbour had been to give the police time to move into position. We later found out that, while we were adrift, the ship had been under close radar scrutiny by the authorities. The two tenders had been spotted as soon as they approached it, and, while they could do nothing about the *Bellatrix*, the DTI instructed the police to intercept the *FourWinds* when it arrived back in England. Ever hopeful of being able to get rid of Caroline for good, the DTI had even booked a berth for the *Ross Revenge* in Harwich once the drifting became apparent, in case help was not forthcoming and we got into trouble, or gave up and sailed into port, as Laser had done.

All I could do was keep on walking and hope that the police would not link me to the others in the van. I passed by nervously, careful to show no obvious interest. The others did not look at me either, knowing that that could draw attention to me. The police assumed that I was a passer-by, and even moved out of my way to let me through.

I got a bus almost immediately and, half an hour later, was in Chicago's house, telling Carol all about the night's events. Ronan phoned soon after I arrived and I filled him in on all the details, including the rapid drifting northwards of his radio ship, and the problems in Ramsgate. He was horrified to learn that the *Bellatrix* had tied up alongside us and caused the *Ross* to drift even faster – and blamed me for not pointing out the hazards of this and stopping it. My protest that I could hardly override the wishes of Willie when Chicago, Watts and Ernie were all on board fell on deaf ears. Ronan had to have someone to blame: as I was on land, and the others were out of his reach, that person was me.

His attitude was frustrating, but not entirely unexpected. Ronan was known for picking a scapegoat for whatever befell the ship, but always forgot about things after a couple of weeks of making the person's life hell. One of the people on board the *Ross* at the time the tower fell down had shot some video footage in the immediate aftermath. The first comment that anyone made on the video as they had looked at the wreckage was not 'What do we do now?' but 'Oh my God – I wonder who the old man is going to blame for this one.'

Luckily for me, but unluckily for Caroline, there was, within hours, an entirely new catastrophe to divert his attention. A message came from Chicago on the ship, via his special telex system. Quite simply, it said that the attempt to erect the new 819 fibreglass aerial system had been a disaster, and that in the process the fibreglass itself may have been damaged. According to his message, there was no chance of getting 819 on the air quickly, and yet more engineering supplies would have to be purchased.

The mast and tuning unit had come to us with instructions and a guarantee that it was entirely self-supporting, even on a ship, and that it required no stays to keep it upright. On erection on the *Ross*, it had bent alarmingly and wobbled constantly from side to side. When the ship rolled, according to Chicago's message, 'It looked like a giant hand waving at passing shipping'. Any attempts to put broadcast power into the mast were doomed to failure, as its electrical properties altered constantly as it changed shape. And there were worries that the stress of the constant flexing could cause damage to the mast's inner workings. Caroline's plans to broadcast on two frequencies on medium wave once more were in ruins, and so the hopes of regular supplies and fuel from the Dutch were dashed. Ronan, however, was optimistic: special stays and equipment would be bought, the mast would be repaired, and the project would go ahead – with a completion date of the end of April.

The *Bellatrix* stayed with the *Ross Revenge* for several days, until a tug arrived to re-anchor the ship. The problem had been at the bottom of the thousand-foot-long anchor chain: the chain was intact, but the anchor had quite simply broken off the bottom link. A new anchor was fitted, and the *Ross* was safe once more. During the few days before the tug's arrival, Peter Phillips could be heard on Caroline. It was strange for me to listen to him, knowing that very shortly he would be gone, never to return.

Once Peter left the ship for the final time, I needed to be back out there to keep things running, and in late April Ronan phoned me to say that a Dutch tender would be leaving from a secret location in twenty-four hours' time. I was to meet him in London the following morning, and he would give me money for records and to pay for travel to the Continent for me and the other new crew, instructions to get to a meeting point with the person running the tender, which apparently would not be the *Bellatrix*.

I spent a happy final night on land, partaking of good freshly cooked food, clean, crisp sheets, and a nice warm bedroom, with hot running water and a bath nearby – none of which I would see again for a while. The next morning, I was sitting in the King's Road eatery which Ronan used as a meeting place for departing crew. Ronan told me that he had some very good news, which would mean a brighter future for the whole organisation. Following nearly two months of broadcasting on short wave, which had in the main been successful, the backers of a proposed religious station in Holland were now willing to rent the airtime on our transmitter.

World Mission Radio, as it would be called, would run twenty hours a day on short wave, with a mixture of bible readings, religious sermons and gospel music, all sent to us pre-recorded onto cassette tapes or three–hour reels. The station was to start on 1 May, and Ronan stressed that as they were paying customers, funding Caroline during a time when the Dutch station was not giving us any revenue, the

WMR broadcasts would have to be run very carefully, with no deviation from schedule, and no dead air if tapes ran out. I was then presented with a large carrier bag full of cassettes and music reels, and told to keep them safe.

Ronan paid me in Swiss francs, so I had no idea how much money I had, but it turned out to be enough to pay the travel expenses and buy about £400 worth of records. I made a mad dash around HMV in Oxford Street, buying as many Top 100 albums and singles as I could afford, and managed to make the Dover train in the nick of time, weighed down with the records, tapes, and other paraphernalia. I met two other crewmembers in Dover, as arranged, and, to my considerable surprise, was allowed through Customs. As the ferry pulled out of Dover, I was finally able to relax and chat to my two comrades. John Bibby was cheerful and excited as usual, and the other person, a new crewmember, Mike Williams, was full of adrenalin, this being the big chance he had been waiting for. In the bar on the ferry, he asked me what a typical six-week stint on Caroline would be like.

I paused before answering, remembering my first stint, when I had been hijacked into presenting programmes by Chicago, and my second, when the crew of the *Ross* had taken arms against a potentially hostile *Bellatrix*. And the most recent one, with the unexpected drifting. I leaned back in my chair, knowing that whatever I could tell him, nothing could prepare him for life on the *Ross Revenge* – a life where weeks of normality or days of excitement could come at any time – and where each new challenge, each new crisis was unexpected, unforeseen, and different from the last.

'Well,' he asked me, 'what's it like?'

'Interesting,' I replied.

10

EIGHTH WONDER

Arriving back on board at the end of April, I was faced with an immediate staff shortage. Everyone on board was long overdue shore leave,
and I had only been able to bring two people out with me. After the
euphoria of getting Caroline back on full power in February, the station was now facing a crisis point: unless other radio services such as
World Mission Radio and the new Dutch station on 819 started bringing in cash soon, we would have a very bleak summer ahead. Already,
we were losing a lot of staff and finding it difficult to recruit new ones,
because the regular pay that Caroline had been able to promise people
in 1987 had simply dried up. I had been lucky in that I had friends willing to put me up and feed me while I was on shore – otherwise, I
would not have been able to survive on what I had been given.

My first priority now was to make a working radio station out of
the few English-speaking people who were on board. Since Chicago
could not be prevailed upon to do programmes, that left myself, John
Bibby and the untried Mike Williams – hardly the sort of team that
superstations are made of. I approached Ad and Erwin, and asked
them if they would like to do programmes on Caroline 558. They
agreed readily – their own station was weeks away from coming on air,
and working for Caroline would help relieve some of the boredom.

I realised that, as the only Caroline presenter with any experience
on board, I would have to do the breakfast programme myself,

something that I had never wanted to do. Breakfast programmes were for the stars of a station, people like Kevin Turner or Mark Matthews, and I simply did not believe I had what it took to be an entertaining breakfast DJ. However, I would have to do it, and that was that.

The staff shortages went on for several weeks, but one day, out of the blue, an English tender arrived, with the people and materials we needed to solve our problems. Peter Moore had done a great job with this tender – as well as the staying material for the fibreglass mast, and two workers to erect it, there were some records, supplies, and two DJs – not novices either, but people who had been on the ship in the past and could be counted on to work well. Steve Masters was one, returning for his third stint, and Keith Francis the other (Keith had been with the ship in 1987 and had left shortly after the mast collapsed).

With Keith and Little Steve on board, the staff shortage was eased considerably, and things were a lot less hectic for all of us. I immediately put Keith Francis onto the breakfast show, Little Steve went onto drivetime, and with Ad and Erwin were still willing to present shows for us, we were now able to run twenty-four hours again.

Work on the fibreglass mast took much longer than expected, but by the end of May it was finally able to transmit, albeit with quite low power, and so we had 819 back on the air again, the ship now boasting two medium wave and one short wave service. A Dutch tender brought news that the 819 signal was reaching well into Holland and the Dutch decided to start their new station the next Monday, 30 May. Because of the length of time 819 had been off since the tower collapsed, and the changes in organisation on the Dutch side, the operation would not be the return of Monique, but the birth of an entirely new Dutch station – Radio 819. Most of the 819 staff, however, would be people who had worked on Monique in the past.

Excitement mounted over the weekend as the new Dutch station prepared to go on the air. Ad Roberts and Erwin Van Der Bliek were back on board, and together with others were rushing around preparing everything for the big day. The ship was busier than it had been for several months. Monday dawned grey and lumpy, with a north-westerly gale whipping the seas around us into a frenzy, and the *Ross* rolling and juddering sharply for the first time since the storms of March.

The Dutch station came on air at 9 AM, with their official opening, and finally our ship was back to normal. For the first time since the collapse of the big tower the previous November, we had Caroline on 558 from Studio 1, and the Dutch next door in Studio 2, pumping out their own programmes on 819. And now we had World Mission Radio on short wave as well, giving the ship a record three simultaneous radio stations, all broadcasting through different aerial arrays. Also, now that 819 was on the air, the Viewpoint religious programmes would be running on medium wave again, after the Dutch closedown at 6 PM. There was a celebratory mood on the ship that morning, Dutch and English alike glad that the long, long winter and spring of struggling with technical problems was behind us. Now, between the Dutch and the religious stations, there would be more than enough money to pay staff, buy new equipment, build up supplies, and generally run things efficiently.

That morning, I was in the galley making coffee, having just done a tape change on World Mission Radio. The ship was obviously turning with the tide, because it started rolling even more violently than it had been before, and I was hard put to keep my footing on the galley floor. We were struck by one particularly violent roll, and there was a sound like a large explosion over my head, somewhere out on the back deck. A series of enormous crashes and bangs reverberated throughout the ship, almost deafening me, and then there was a peculiar noise, rather like a giant pencil rolling around on the back deck . . .

I shot outside, and climbed the ladder to the back deck, looking in horror at the sight that greeted me. The fibreglass mast had snapped in two a third of the way up, and part of the top section was in the water, with more of it rolling back and forth across the deck and getting tangled up in stays. The greater part of it lay ruined on the deck, broken and twisted, and charred in places from electrical overloading. The months of work that had gone into it were wasted. Radio 819 was off the air less than three hours after its birth, and now there was no possibility of getting anything on at all.

Luckily for us, the fall of the 819 mast had not damaged the main towers carrying the 558 and short wave aerials, so Caroline and WMR were all right, but we knew that the loss of the Dutch station, after so much money had been invested in it, would have far-reaching consequences. Mike Watts examined the broken mast and pointed out the massive internal damage it had sustained. It had literally burnt away from the inside while it had been on air, hence the break. This had been while it was running only a tenth of the manufacturer's promised load through it.

Early June saw us finally having success in recruiting new presenters, with the arrival on board of a contingent of crew from the Israeli pirate radio, The Voice of Peace. The first to arrive, and by far the most difficult to deal with, was Dave Asher. Many months previously, when Coconut had been on board, he had told me all about Asher, describing him as 'the wild man of the *Peace* ship' and telling me that I would find it impossible to get him to work within the format, or to conform to the presentation guidelines. Asher arrived from Ramsgate in early June, in the middle of the night, on *FourWinds*. Seeing him standing on the deck of the *Ross*, wrapped up in a duffel coat against the cold, looking small, innocent and utterly harmless, it was hard to imagine him as the wild man of anywhere. His face betrayed surprise and hurt when he was told that, like any new presenter, he would start out on the overnight programme. Once in the studio, however, his mild personality was replaced by that of a zany extrovert who excelled in all the clichés and bad habits of the 'local radio DJ' style that Caroline tried so hard to avoid. There were silly voices, impersonations of famous people, stupid features and manic laughter – all in his first programme.

I took him aside the next day and asked him if he had read the presentation guidelines. 'Of course I have,' he replied, turning his wounded and innocent look on me. 'I haven't broken them, have I?'

Getting Dave to work within the Caroline format was like breaking in a wild horse – he tried every trick in the book and continued using strange accents and uttering almost incomprehensible links between records long after he had been told to stop. The silly thing was that his natural speaking voice was lovely, but no one got to hear it because of his 'style'. So, on the overnight spot he stayed. Actually, his style of broadcasting may have worked very well elsewhere, and I felt guilty in some ways making him quieten down, thinking that I might be stifling real talent. However, if he wanted to get on in radio, he would have to learn to fit in with the 'house style' of wherever he worked, so my constant breathing down his neck was for his own good. At least, to salve my conscience, that's what I hoped.

A little while after Dave, two more ex-Voice of Peace presenters, Ian Macc and Neil Gates, arrived. Ian was a godsend to me – an excellent presenter, and a true professional, determined to make it to the very top. I soon promoted him to drivetime, to replace Little Steve, who had just left. Neil was very different from Ian, much quieter in his approach, and a more basic 'no frills' presenter, but he too was a godsend. He settled into the night-time programme and was soon producing excellent programmes, seeming to know instinctively what I wanted for that particular slot. Neil soon impressed me in other ways too – he was the soul of helpfulness around the ship, willing to do anything for anyone, and never complained when the workload got tough. Whatever you asked him to do, he would just do it: no complaints, no questions, no postponement.

Socially, Neil was very extrovert, in contrast to Ian, who was all talk on air, and very quiet off it. The two of them made such a contrast that they really enlivened life aboard the *Ross*. Neil showed a lot of interest in the day-to-day running of the format and the administration, and was always offering to give me a hand if I was tired or worked out.

On land, plans were afoot to buy tower sections to build a much bigger twin-tower system than we currently had on the ship. The idea was that this, together with money for new components provided by World Mission Radio, would allow Chicago to diplex our signal again – that is, to have both 558 and 819 running through the same aerial.

But by the end of June, no progress had been made, and the Dutch were threatening to pull out of Caroline altogether. The Dutch crew were removed from the ship at the end of June, but then, puzzlingly, brought back again a few days later. When we asked them what was going on in their organisation, they couldn't, or wouldn't, tell us.

11

MADNESS

JULY–DECEMBER 1988

I was wakened from a deep sleep by Mike Watts shaking me in my bunk. I groaned and turned round to face him, blinking in the light, and struggled to wake up. Looking at my watch, I saw it was a quarter to midnight, bang in the middle of my eight-hour sleep period. This had better be good, I thought to myself, and then noticed that Mike not only had a serious expression on his face but had brought me down a cup of tea. Whatever it was, it was not going to be good. Mike never woke anyone up with tea. Ever.

Mike waited for a few moments while I sat up in bed, and gulped down the first few mouthfuls of tea, to bring myself to full wakefulness. 'I'm really sorry to wake you up at this time, Steve,' he said, 'but I've had some news from land, and I thought you should be the first to know, so that we can handle it together.'

'We have to give 558 to the Dutch – Chicago called and told me about it a few minutes ago. Ronan tried to hold them off as long as he could, and promised them a new mast and 819 by August, but they told him they want to be on the air now, or else.'

Mike continued: 'I know how you feel, Steve, but we've got to do it – otherwise we lose the Dutch for good, including the fuel tenders and everything else. I feel just as disappointed as you do after all the work we've done getting Caroline back on its feet again, but according

151

to Chicago the new mast will be built very soon, and by the end of the summer the Dutch will have 819, and we can have 558 back again.'

I was reeling with shock and disappointed that, after the whole spring of hard work recovering from Caroline's winter of low power, we were now about to lose our airtime, but I realised that Chicago and Ronan were right. We would have to let the Dutch take our place on 558, make the best of it, and hope that the new antenna system was built quickly.

Mike went on to tell me that the Dutch backers wanted to be on the air within forty-eight hours or they would pull out: we would have only one more day of broadcasting before they took over our frequency. The Dutch station would initially broadcast from 6 AM to 6 PM English time, leaving us with the evening and overnight for Caroline. We talked about it as I dressed, quickly working out how best to work out details of the transfer, how to notify our listeners that we were gone, and what to do between us for the rest of the night. We had just one day of daytime broadcasting left to tell our listeners that we were going night-time only but would be back in eight weeks or so: I would have to script, produce and air announcements to be played throughout the whole of that day.

I left Cabin 2 and headed along the corridor to where the Dutch programme controller, Erwin, slept. I was thinking ruefully that once again Caroline had surprised me in my sleep and life on board the ship was about to enter a whole different phase. I knocked on Erwin's door, and let myself in with Mike, thinking that at least I wasn't the only one who would lose his beauty sleep that night. I explained to Erwin what was going on, and he told me that he had been expecting this, as it was what our owner had promised the Dutch bosses on land before they had come out. I then explained that I was about to tell the rest of our crew, and that we would try to make the handover to the new Dutch daytime service as smoothly as possible.

I then went round the ship, and collared the Caroline crew one by one, asking them to go to the messroom, where Mike and I would be making an important announcement. With the others all assembled, I took the floor, standing up against the dartboard on the messroom wall, looking at their expectant faces. Over the next few minutes, I watched the expressions on those faces swing between surprise, shock, anger and, finally, resigned acceptance. After I had filled them in on what was going on, I reassured them that the situation would only be temporary, and that Caroline would return to daytime broadcasting later in the summer, possibly by the end of August, as soon as the two new bigger masts had been built, and Chicago had been given the equipment needed to broadcast on two separate frequencies. Now, of course, we would be overstaffed – a very unusual situation. We sat around and talked for an hour or so, discussing the various issues that the Dutch takeover of 558 would bring up. Caroline presenters would become entirely nocturnal for a while – though someone would still have to be up during the day to run the World Mission Radio tapes.

The English crew of the *Ross Revenge* were not too annoyed with the Dutch for taking over our airtime, but they were irked by the fact that we would still have to be available during the day to do the menial tasks on board, while the Dutch DJs, who were paid about £200 a week by their bosses, got away with doing little or nothing on board. As someone pointed out, although the Dutch were paid to run their station, we were the ones who had got 558 on the air by building masts at sea with our bare hands, so why should we be relegated to the dark hours?

After a while, I had to excuse myself and get to work: Keith Francis had left a couple of weeks before, so I was back on the breakfast programme, and had to have everything in place by 5 AM. Caroline was running twenty-four hours at this stage, but news of the forthcoming changes was embargoed until 5 AM, to give me time to record proper announcements and prepare information sheets to which presenters could refer when talking about what was going on. It was very important that our listeners got the message that, although we would not be on in the daytime anymore, they could still listen to us at night, and that if they were prepared to wait a month or so, they would have us back in the daytime as well.

For once, we would be completely honest with our listeners, explaining that the Dutch station was needed on air to 'pay the rent' and that Caroline would have to take a back seat until bigger masts and more powerful equipment could be obtained. In our announcements, we estimated that it would be six to eight weeks before 819 could come on the air and the Dutch could move off 558.

And so, at 5 AM on 8 July 1988, I took to the air for what was to be Radio Caroline's last breakfast programme for quite some time. I started the programme with a few tracks and hints of a forthcoming major announcement and, at 5.15, I played the first of the pre-recorded announcements, and the news was out – Caroline would become a night-time only station from the next day and a new Dutch station, Radio 558, would be on the air daily from 6 AM to 6 PM. The announcements were aired at quarter past, half past, and quarter to the hour for maximum effect, as we had such a short time to tell people what was going on. Also, news bulletins at the top of the hour carried the story in more detail, and presenters were instructed to mention it from time to time as well.

Just as the breakfast programme was drawing to a close, less than four hours after the first announcement of the new Dutch station, a large Dutch navel vessel appeared out of the mist, and started circling around us, apparently inspecting and photographing the *Ross Revenge*. They remained in the vicinity of the Falls Head for most of the morning and made several close passes, heading off at around lunchtime. Obviously the Dutch authorities were aware of the forthcoming Dutch pirate and wanted up-to-date surveillance photos of the *Ross Revenge* to hand when they were discussing what to do about it.

Throughout the morning, I was hard at work in the newsroom, revising schedules, printing playlists and sorting out the many things which would need to be altered before the new system came into operation. I worked out a system of three-hour airshifts that would give those remaining a fair share of the overnight airtime and a rota for the WMR tape-minding. Finally, by lunchtime, everything was sorted out and, after the final lunchtime news at 1 PM, I went down to the mess-room to watch *Neighbours*.

The arrival of the tender from England later that day meant that we could solve our overstaffing problems before the shorter days began. Conveniently, both Rob and I had now filled our airshifts for that day, so we would not be missed. I had a last few minutes of rushing around, making sure that Ian Macc and Mike Watts were aware of everything I wanted them to do, and then I was onto the fishing boat, and heading away for what I decided would be a good long break on shore.

Waking up early the next morning, I was just in time to hear Caroline closing down and the Dutch-language Radio 558 taking to the air for the first time. In PM's office later that morning, there wasn't a happy face to be seen anywhere.

Ronan came over when he heard I was there, and we had a long chat. He promised me that getting the Dutch on air would bring in more money and help Caroline attain the same high standards it had reached in 1987. There would be money for new equipment, better facilities and regular supplies – and even regular pay for the presenters too. I told him to be sure to stick to that, as without pay we could never hope to keep bright new presenters such as Ian Macc or Neil Gates with us.

For my own needs, I decided to take a temporary job while on shore. The ever-helpful John Burch quickly set me up selling tickets for bus sightseeing tours near Piccadilly Circus.

The weeks passed quickly. Now that I was earning money, I was able once more to have decent clothes, shoes with no holes in them, and a feeling of belonging to humanity. You do without many things on board ship, and I never ceased to be surprised at the fact that on land there was always hot water, reliable electricity and food shops just around the corner.

After a few weeks, I spoke to Ronan, who told me that, as nighttime-only Caroline 'didn't matter', I should remain on land a little while longer, save some more money, and return to the ship about two weeks before 819 got going. On the 819 front, progress was slow: the mast sections were being purchased and moved to coastal locations for transport out to the ship. Construction of the new mega-towers would obviously take some time, but we now had enough money from the WMR religious service to enable Chicago to buy components for a diplexer, so he could work on this in advance of the new masts being built. John's job with the bus company came in useful in providing transport for the new mast sections. Arriving in a harbour with a lorry-load of mast sections would almost certainly prompt official enquiry and discovery, but John hit on the clever idea of loading the sections onto the upstairs of an open-top sightseeing bus, in which they were invisible from ground level. The arrival of a sightseeing bus in a coastal town in high summer would attract very little attention.

By September I had undone the worst of the financial damage that a year working for Caroline had wreaked on me. I now had a little money in the bank and a cheap but reliable second-hand car. I was more or less ready to go back out to the ship and spend the better part of the autumn and winter there, knowing that at least I now had a little security.

With Caroline still just on overnights until the work was completed, my working hours became quite fragmented when I returned to the ship. Unlike the other Caroline presenters, I couldn't sleep throughout the daylight hours, as I had to be available for the Monique international news at 3.30 PM – which in practice involved getting up no later than 2.30 PM to have time to prepare. Generally, I would go to bed straight after the 8.30 AM international news in the morning, sleep through to 2.30 PM, and then remain up for twelve hours until I had finished my night-time show on Caroline, after which I would grab another few hour's sleep, until around 7 AM, and the start of the cycle again.

With just three of us on board for Caroline programmes, we settled into an easy-going routine quite quickly, with Chris on first, from early evening through to 11 PM, me following between 11 and 2 AM, and Little Steve on between 2 and 5.30 AM, when he would hand over 558 to the Dutch. It was the first time in ages that I had presented programmes so late at night, and I found it immensely satisfying.

Many DJs believe that they have to work their way steadily through the time slots on a radio station, with the ultimate aim of getting on the breakfast show. To them, demotion into the middle of the night is traumatic and ego-deflating. With me, although I had by now worked in every Caroline time slot, I never minded what I was doing, and would just as happily broadcast in the middle of the night as do a breakfast or drive show.

In fact, I found the overnight programme more satisfying than those during the daytime – there was a certain magic to sitting in that studio in the middle of the night, playing music and looking out across the dark sea to the distant lights of land. Night-time audiences are far smaller than daytime ones, but somehow this makes for a more personal, even intimate, connection between presenter and listener. It seemed to me that the people who were driving through the night, or working a night shift, or at home, unable to sleep, valued Caroline more than those who had it on in the background during the hustle and bustle of a busy day. The ship would be beautifully peaceful at night, and I would dim the studio lights as far as was practical, and revel in the atmosphere that the location and the music created.

Luckily we no longer had to sit up all day running World Mission Radio: the religious backers now paid for someone to be sent out to the ship especially to do this. One such person, who arrived on a Dutch tender not long after I came back, was Tobias, who was also to be our on-board cook. During my eighteen months with Caroline I had encountered many cooks on board the *Ross* – some bad, like Penny from my first stint, some rapidly improving, like John Bibby, and some truly excellent such as Kevin Turner, who could not be beaten in the galley. Tobias, however, was a whole new experience for me.

A few days of Tobias's cooking set the crew on course for an almost outright rebellion. His method of 'cooking' involved putting something into a large, deep roasting tray, filled up to the brim with cooking oil, fat and grease. Meat, veg, potatoes would all go into this grease-bath, where they would be cooked for about twenty minutes on a low heat, and served up in a slop of fatty mess, meat oozing blood, potatoes still solid.

Protests from everyone resulted in Tobias merely extending the cooking time from twenty minutes to half an hour, but on a lower heat. The resultant slop was just as inedible, and day after day passed with entire meals being left uneaten by almost the whole crew. Chicago eventually dropped Tobias from the cooking duties altogether, declaring it a waste of good food, and the English DJs from then on took turns cooking, leaving Tobias with just his World Mission Radio duties. Unfortunately for all concerned, he didn't seem much good at these either, and Chicago frequently upbraided him after coming across the WMR studio silent, the tape or music reel having run out, and Tobias having done nothing about it. Eventually, he caused so many gaps in transmission on the service that he had to be taken off this too. And so the English crew had to take over the job again, unpaid – unlike Tobias, who was paid to cook and to run WMR, but who was incapable of doing either.

Having taken Tobias off cooking and WMR duties, Chicago thought that his capacity to disrupt normal life on the ship would now be minimised, but this was not to be, as we found out over dinner one evening. I had cooked that night and we were all sitting around the messroom table tucking into some nice roast chicken.

Tobias pushed his plate aside and began to speak, his English broken but his words impossible to ignore.

'People . . . I have something I think I need to tell you,' he began. Conversation around the table quietened down, but we all continued to eat. 'Last night . . . I lie in my bunk . . . and I am looking at, how you say it, my private parts – I am holding them and looking.' There was dead silence in the mess room now, forks poised halfway to mouths. 'I see little creatures,' said Tobias. 'Little animals crawling all over my private parts.' He paused, but there was no response from anyone. 'I just tell you about my animals, in case it happens that I give them to you.' And Tobias got up and left the room.

The room exploded into conversation as soon as he left. One of the Dutch crew, who shared a double cabin with Tobias, then asked Chicago if he could move into an unoccupied English cabin. Chicago agreed, and watched with a twinkle in his eye the conversation that rapidly developed between the rest of us about whether it was possible that we could catch Tobias's 'animals' through normal daily contact, such as brushing past him in the corridor or sitting on the toilet.

Chicago dryly informed us that, yes, we could catch Tobias's crabs from the toilet seat, and took malicious pleasure in pointing out that since the seats were black, it wouldn't do any good looking for them before we sat down.

'Well, he's been on here a week, and we haven't caught anything from him yet,' said Little Steve. 'We'd notice if we picked them up, wouldn't we?'

'Not necessarily,' said Chicago, grinning at the young DJ's obvious discomfort.

It wasn't just Little Steve who suddenly felt uncomfortable – we all started feeling itchy, and doubtless everyone wanted to slip away and quietly check their pubic regions, but no one wanted to be the first to do so. Chicago stood up, grabbed his mug to go to the galley for some tea, and left us with one of his typically unsettling remarks.

'There's nothing to worry about,' he told us. 'There was an outbreak on the *Mi Amigo* once, and it was quite simple to get rid of.'

He went out the door, doing his usual trick of ducking his head back in to deliver a parting shot: 'All you have to do is shave all your pubic hair off and wash the area in petrol twice a day, for a week. I've got some petrol down in the generator room, if anybody needs it.'

After that, everyone gave Tobias a wide berth – and, to just to be on the safe side, his unfortunate ex-cabin-mate as well. And I started using a toilet in a disused engineer's cabin, one that I was sure Tobias didn't know about.

After several weeks of tinkering, Chicago finished his technical work, and on 16 October the ship came on the air with two clear signals, on 558 and 819. This time it would work – we were using old-fashioned tried-and-tested technology, and our self-erected masts, which had withstood the previous winter's gales. The Dutch immediately began publicising their frequency change to 819, to take place in three week's time. For the moment they would be on both 819 and 558 during the day, but from 6 November, at midday, they would be on 819 only, and we would have 558 back at last. There was an immediate air of euphoria on board the ship, as now our future was secure once more, and of course the Viewpoint programmes were started in the evenings on

819, which would bring in more revenue. On Caroline, we celebrated the news by launching a countdown of the number of days left to full transmissions. Before we knew it, the countdown was into single figures, with nine days to go, eight days, seven, six . . .

The sixth of November came quickly, and at 11 AM (midday in Holland), the Dutch relinquished 558 kHz and renamed themselves Radio 819, as had been originally intended all those months ago. And Caroline was back on the air on 558 – twenty-four hours a day. I started off the daytime programmes with an hour of continuous music, and then Steve Masters did the first regular programme at noon English time, commencing with a record I had selected specially for the occasion: Helen Shapiro's 'Walking Back to Happiness'. Not long after our programmes began, a dot on the horizon appeared – it turned out to be the fishing boat, bringing supplies, letters from land and, most importantly, more staff: now that we were running twenty-four hours, we would need more.

Among the new arrivals on the tender were Nigel Harris, who had done stints with Caroline on and off for many years, Canadian DJ Judy Murphy, and an American called Chuck, who was big, jovial and slightly puzzled-looking. The source of his puzzlement soon became obvious – he had been recruited by Ronan himself, who in his efforts to sell the idea of Caroline to him, had told Chuck that the ship was the last word in luxury cruisers, with a swimming pool, gym, and steward service in all cabins. The rusty-red *Ross Revenge* was not exactly what he had been expecting, but he took it good-naturedly, and retired to his non-serviced cabin to get some sleep, returning upstairs only briefly, to make a forlorn enquiry about the ship's laundry service. Ronan had told him that if he left his dirty washing outside his cabin door at night, it would be returned, cleaned and ironed by 7 AM!

We now had a good contrast of styles and voices. The end result sounded better than I could have expected – and it was even better when we were joined by Ian Macc and Dave Asher a few weeks later.

Ian went straight onto the breakfast show, where he proved that Radio Caroline could sound ten times better than any land-based station if it had the right staff, attitude and equipment. He put a lot of creativity, energy and sheer professionalism into his show, and as the newsreader, I found it great fun to be a part of his breakfast routine. Judy Murphy was on after Ian; her relaxed and professional style fitted well into Caroline's mid-morning mood. Dave Asher, now sounding very good, did afternoons, Nigel Harris the drivetime show. It was possibly the best presenter line-up that Caroline had had in my entire time as programme controller, and a real sign that, with our troubles behind us, we were capable of recruiting and holding on to good people once more. The arrival back on board in December of Neil Gates was to make things better still.

Social life was good on the ship too – it was always better with at least one woman on board, as people seemed to be more open and relaxed in a mixed-gender society. We had some marvellous nights in the messroom during those late November storms, and one night when things were calmer, we came up with an idea that proved to be the simplest, yet most fun, thing that had happened on board the ship for a long time – a massive game of hide-and-seek, involving the whole crew and spanning the entire vessel – played with the lights out. The fifty-six rooms, and hundreds of nooks and crannies on board the *Ross*, would make the game truly challenging and, with most of the lights off, the ship would be an atmospheric – and even frightening – place. We didn't turn all the lights off, of course – the outside ones needed to be left on so that other vessels could see us at anchor, but indoors was plunged into complete darkness, with the exception of the studio, where Tony Kirk was on air, keeping Caroline going through his night-shift, while the rest of us had fun. He had been less enthusiastic about the game anyway, so didn't feel that he was missing much.

The first searcher waited in the messroom, counting to a hundred while we secreted ourselves all over the ship, and then came looking for us with a torch. I hid at first in the air-conditioning cupboard, but soon changed my mind and left it, as crouching still in a room where ice-cold air from outside was sucked in before being piped to the cabins soon froze me stiff. My second hiding place was in the news-room, crouched on a worktop behind the news-room door. I remained crouched in this position for almost an hour before I was discovered, by which time I

161

was so cramped that it was a relief to be able to move.

It was now my turn to seek out the hidden, and I crept around the ship, keeping my torch off, and walking in bare feet so that no one would hear my approach. Gliding down through the stairways and catwalks of the engine room, I soon stood in a patch of thick, greasy engine oil, and decided that my footwear policy had been a mistake. The whole ship was eerie in the darkness, the engine room even more so, with its multiple levels, sloping passageways, ladders and catwalks. Way down below the waterline, you could hear the sea sloshing gently against the hull all around you. I crept towards the mechanical engineering stores, looking for any signs of hidden life.

I thought I heard the faintest of noises from the store room, and snapped on my torch, being rewarded by the sight of someone's bottom poking out of a cupboard. The bottom stayed perfectly still as I approached it, its owner obviously not realising that part of him was sticking out from his hiding place. I gave it a smack, and there was a muffled curse as Nigel Harris leapt in fright, only to bang his head off the top of the metal cupboard that he had been trying to hide in.

Nigel then took over from me, and I went away to hide once more, while he counted in the messroom. I then had what I considered to be a brilliant idea, and concealed myself once more in the air-conditioning cupboard, which was on the main corridor, close to the messroom door. When I heard Nigel leave the messroom, and walk past me to the upper levels of the ship, I slipped out, doubled back, and shot into the messroom itself – the one place he would never think of looking in. Diving under the messroom table, I slid into a narrow space underneath the long bench seat that backed up against the wall and found myself on top of Ian Macc. I was obviously not the first person to discover this hiding place. Soon, things became even more interesting – as Dave Asher, who was hiding himself again after a spell as hunter, doubled back into the messroom, and flung himself under our bench seat, landing in surprise on top of Ian and me. Now it really was crowded under the table, a surprised hunter caught three people in one go. The game continued until well after midnight, and ended up with tea and snacks in the messroom, the whole crew feeling very united and relaxed. It was a night that was talked about with fondness for many months afterwards, though we never got around to repeating the game again.

With Caroline back on full time, I was keen to update our long-running Lotto 6/49 adverts, which had started in 1985 and had been running unchanged since 1986. The same two or three adverts were rotated, one every hour of every day, and the listeners had grown heartily sick of them, to judge by the mail we were receiving on the subject. I got together with Judy, Neil and some of the others and suggested that we each script a new Lotto advert and then pool our efforts to produce five or six new versions to update the campaign. My contribution featured a conversation between Judy and myself, with background music by Alison Moyet, 'That Old Devil Called Love Again'. Judy was asking me why I loved her, running through her good features and getting a negative response from me each time. At the end of the ad, it was revealed that I loved her because she had just won a million dollars on the Canadian state lottery.

Several other versions featured other members of the crew, Judy being used more than once, thanks to her charming voice and excellent acting skills. They started airing towards the middle of December, at around the time a tender arrived to take Judy away from us – she was going back to her native Canada for Christmas. Before she left, I got her to record a special programme on tape which I now had, so she would be part of the Caroline line-up at Christmas too.

December became wild and stormy, and before long we began to experience food shortages, not having had a Dutch tender for several weeks. We were running low on essential items such as tea, milk, sugar and meat, and the fresh-water supplies on board were rapidly dwindling. So when the Belgian tender *Polstar* showed up one Wednesday evening, we were very pleased indeed, and happy to assist Willie as he nudged it alongside, and tied up to our port side. That happy mood soon turned to disappointment, anger and outright rebellion, though. We couldn't believe our ears when Willie told us that this was the last tender before Christmas and, more importantly, that it had not brought us any fresh water. Our water stocks were so low after weeks without a visit from the Dutch that we were bound to run dry soon, and yet they had not even bothered to bring us this precious commodity, which cost almost nothing compared to the fuel they were pumping aboard. The food supplies from the *Polstar* were also virtually non-existent. It looked as if we were going to be in for a very bleak Christmas.

When we complained, we got a rough ride from the Dutch station boss, Nico, over the fact that the 819 transmitter had been off the air for half a day earlier in the month. He insisted that we had simply been too lazy to switch it back on after a minor breakdown, and would not listen when Mike told him that the transmitter had blown a valve, which had taken some time to replace.

Looking at our food and water supplies, it was obvious that we would run out of most things, most critically water, long before Christmas. En masse, we confronted Willie and Nico and demanded that something come sooner.

Tempers flared when the Dutch branded Caroline and its staff a waste of time which sucked up the profits from their operation. For a few moments, it looked as if the entire English crew was going to walk off the ship in protest.

Despite Nico's bluster, the Dutch could not run the *Ross Revenge* on their own, and they knew it. The 'waste of time' Caroline crew, apart from running the station which owned the vessel, did all the engineering, cleaning and maintenance duties on board. Without us, the Dutch station would not be on the air for long.

In the end, we drafted a stinking letter, signed by everyone on the Caroline side, which Ian Macc would bring back to land and show to Ronan. The letter stated that after rebuilding the towers with our bare hands and getting World Mission Radio, Radio 819 and Viewpoint 819 on the air, we expected to be treated better than we were. We didn't mind the poor pay, or the isolation of being on-board ship, but felt that the least that the management could do, given all the money we were bringing in for them, was to keep us fed and watered. We all added our signatures to the letter and Ian took it on to the *Polstar*, which sailed away just before midnight, leaving behind a ship simmering with resentment.

As December went by, the supply situation on board the *Ross* became worse, with hardly any food or water left. We were back to eating tinned and dried food from the emergency supply in the stores, and the fresh-water taps were giving us a brownish sludge from the bottom of the tanks, which had to be filtered and boiled before it could be used for anything. Making a cup of tea now became a lengthy experience. Eventually, we ran out of tea and milk as well.

As Christmas week came, it was obvious that our letter had been ignored, and that there would be no tender before Christmas. Our last carton of long-life milk was held back in reserve, along with the last of our meat – some tinned sausages – for Christmas Day, so we would at least have milk in our coffee and something other than rice or soup to celebrate with. With our morale plummeting, we decided that what was needed was some way of turning our disillusion into something more positive.

Not long before Christmas, there had been a terrible train crash at Clapham Junction, with many people killed and injured. I had, of course, reported on it extensively in Caroline's news bulletins, feeling a bit of a ghoul, as all journalists must, at making my daily business out of reporting such tragedy, and wishing that there was something I could do to help. The idea we came up with was for Caroline to raise money for the disaster fund which had been set up for the injured and bereaved by running a sponsored fast on 23 December. As well as raising money for charity, this might provoke some feelings of guilt amongst our organisation on land. The others were very enthusiastic about the scheme.

At the stroke of midnight on 22 December, the eating stopped, and we had our first fast report on 558. The following day, there were regular reports throughout the breakfast show of how we were coping without food; these carried on through the day and into the evening. Constant appeals were made for listeners to send money to the Clapham fund, and we were told later that quite a bit was received by the fund, in letters marked 'Radio Caroline/Clapham Disaster Fund'.

Apart from the Dutch, who were not taking part in the event, only one person was caught by the 'Food Police' and shamed on air. Tony

Kirk was spotted sneaking down to his cabin with a guilty look on his face, and was caught red-handed a few minutes later having a sneaky snack behind closed doors. Everyone else resisted temptation, despite the hunger pangs. Just after midnight, we reported live on the end of the fast, and the crew pigging out – not mentioning the fact that the only thing left in the food stores to pig out on was bread and jam.

Christmas Eve dawned with still no sign of a tender, though hopes were high that there would be one during the day, as the sea was calm. Surely they wouldn't leave us without proper supplies over Christmas?

Christmas Eve drew to a close and, as darkness fell over the Falls Head once more, we realised that this year there would be no magic Christmas tender. Mike laid the table for the Christmas dinner of rice and tinned sausages that he would turn into something really special the following day, and the sole remaining carton of milk was taken out of its hiding place and put on the table, for white coffee on Christmas morning. Dave Asher and I stayed out on the bridge for a while, watching forlornly for any lights, and then we drifted off to bed, all hope of tendering forgotten.

I was wakened sometime just before dawn by the clamour of the tender bell, and a knock on my cabin door. I dressed and emerged out on deck at high speed, eager to see what was heading our way. Dave the Fish was just tying up alongside in the *FourWinds*, and on board the fishing boat I could make out the forms of Dave himself . . . and Peter Moore. Peter climbed aboard as supplies began to be passed across from the boat, including tea, milk, bread, meat and fresh vegetables. There was also a turkey and a Christmas tree. So, we would have Christmas after all!

Mike Watts got busy in the galley preparing the turkey, and I went on the air for my Christmas Day programme, including, at 12.30, a Caroline message of thanks to all our supporters. Exactly like a year before, Christmas Day saw the *Ross Revenge* in the midst of a sea so calm that not even a ripple broke the surface. Again, nature seemed to be smiling on us. Outside on deck, the atmosphere was one of peace and tranquillity – indoors, it was all bustle, excitement and Christmas cheer.

We had a really enjoyable evening, with good food, wine, sparkling conversation, and plenty of treats. John and Anita Burch and Jenny Knight of the Caroline Movement had done us proud with the supplies on the tender, which had been bought or donated thanks to the many aardvarks who were members of the organisation.

On Boxing Day, the *Polstar* turned up and came alongside on our port deck to pump fuel and the much-needed fresh water on board. Also on board the *Polstar* were the remaining sections of the big new towers that we had purchased and had talked about building the previous summer. Most of these sections had been delivered months ago but had never been erected. We were still using the twin-tower system, including the old cod-liver-oil pipe, which we had built a year ago. Now, apparently, there was movement from the management on land to get the new, bigger and taller masts built, so that we could eventually broadcast with more power on both frequencies.

New Year's Eve saw us airing the special programme which had been recorded in advance by Judy Murphy, who we now knew was not coming back. We announced it as a special last programme that she had recorded to express her thanks to Caroline and its supporters. She would be starting a job on Radio Luxembourg only two days later, and was probably already over there preparing for it. Immediately after Judy's tape came to an end, I made a live announcement, accompanied by Neil and Nigel, thanking her for the work she had done for Caroline.

Then I started into the Top 100 tracks of the year, as chosen by the Caroline crew. This countdown took several hours, and ended with the Pet Shop Boys' 'Domino Dancing' being announced as the most popular record on board for 1988. After me, I scheduled Nigel Harris, with the best album tracks of '88, and then it was me again, joined by everyone else, with the traditional New Year's Eve Caroline Party. This was the most ambitious day of special programming that I had planned to date, and it seemed to go down very well with everyone on board.

Nineteen-eighty-eight had been a long and often difficult year, with many setbacks, but it looked as if things were far better now than they had been twelve months previously, and we had every reason to believe that 1989 would see things getting better still.

12

SPARKS

Nineteen-eighty-nine started on the *Ross Revenge* with a flurry of mast-building, as the new taller towers began to take shape at either end of the ship. Mostly this was achieved without any interruption to our existing transmissions, though we occasionally switched off for brief periods as we hauled sections skywards.

A welcome sign that the station was doing better came in the shape of the huge salvage tug which appeared out of the mist one morning to bring us the largest delivery of fuel, food and water we had ever seen. Every fuel tank on the *Ross* was filled until we were laden down with a quarter of a million litres of diesel, and the entire fresh-water plumbing system was flushed out for several hours before being re-filled with crystal-clear drinking water. So much food was delivered that the cans of drink and tinned foods filled the cold store and were stacked in the corridor at the back of the ship. This was real evidence that the effort we had made to get both the short wave and the Dutch stations on the air was finally paying off.

The unexpected arrival of the tug produced one of the best-ever 'Mike Watts moments', and one that we were to tease him about for months afterwards. As the tug had come alongside, and ropes were being thrown across, Nik Jackson, a recently arrived DJ, on his first ever week at sea, fumbled and dropped one of them. 'You stupid bloody idiot,' Mike roared at him. 'Haven't you ever tied up a salvage tug before?'

We fell about the place laughing at this, which made Mike even more annoyed.

Nik was a real find for us: a quiet and serious young man who quickly developed into a really polished and professional-sounding broadcaster, easily as good as Ian Macc. It was easy to see that he would have a good career in broadcasting, and we were just grateful that we were now stable enough to attract someone with his level of talent once more.

As well as new recruits, now that Caroline was back on its feet we were having some success in attracting back previous presenters. Caroline Martin, who had previously broadcast on the ship before my time, returned to us that spring. She was both a great presenter and a source of much frustration to the male crew members, whom she teased relentlessly, even after beginning a shipboard romance with Dave Asher. And I was delighted to welcome back Coconut, who had been with us a year previously, during the dark days after the fall of the big tower.

At the same time, another new service was started from the ship, using the silent hours on the 819 transmitter between the end of religious programming at 11 PM and the start of the Dutch broadcasts at 4 AM. Named 'Caroline 819 – The Overnight Alternative', it played rockier music, with more album tracks and new releases than 558, and was programmed by Rob Harrison, who in a little under a year with Caroline had greatly impressed everyone with his skills in the studio and the galley, and in mast-climbing.

During a break on land at the end of January, PM, John Burch and I did a lot of talking about how the Caroline Movement could help the station celebrate its twenty-fifth birthday in style. We came up with the idea of holding an aardvark convention on board one of the Olau Line ferries over the Easter weekend. The ferry would have disco, bar and food facilities, and would enable many hundreds of people to pass close to the *Ross Revenge* and see it in comfort and safety. John Burch had always run safe sightseeing trips, of course, but the sheer numbers wanting to come at Easter would be beyond the capability of any small vessel. We agreed on a package which would give the fans a return cruise on the *Olau Britannia*, passing the *Ross Revenge* twice, with a Caroline disco, a meal, and the opportunity to meet staff not currently on board the *Ross* itself.

I returned to the ship in February to start work on preparations for the Easter celebration. During the weeks leading up to Easter, press interest in the twenty-fifth anniversary began to grow, and we had a number of journalists visiting the ship on tenders or special sightseeing boats. The BBC also indicated that they wanted to run a feature on Caroline's birthday, with content and interviews filmed on board the *Ross Revenge*.

We had been told by our CB contact that the BBC would want to interview three of us, and it was decided that myself, Mike Watts and whoever happened to be on air when they arrived would be the ones to go in front of the cameras. Caroline Martin gave me a quick haircut, Mike smartened himself up, and Rob Harrison wandered around the ship in his trendiest clothes. It was an ideal day at the Falls Head, one of the first hot sunny days of spring, with calm seas and good visibility. Eventually a dot was spotted heading towards us, and soon proved to be the ever-reliable Dave the Fish, his little boat, the *Four-Winds*, loaded to maximum capacity, with the BBC crew, cameras, lighting and sound equipment.

The *FourWinds* tied up alongside us, and the BBC made a short film of the 'Daytime Live' presenter Simon Potter climbing aboard. They then all got on board themselves, and introduced themselves to us. The BBC, still highly unionised and subject to certain restrictive practices, had decided they needed a twelve-strong film crew to shoot the ship and interview its staff. We watched in astonishment as cameraman, assistant cameraman, lighting man and assistant, sound man and assistant, make-up girl and assistant, producer, director and assistant all came on board – and finally, unbelievably, a union representative sent to make sure that everyone did only what they were supposed to do and that no one was asked to do anything the union didn't approve of. Amazed as we were at this display of force (the BBC had brought as many people to record one fifteen-minute piece as we had on board to run Caroline 558, Caroline 819, Dutch Radio 819, Viewpoint and World Mission Radio all together), we said nothing and let them get on with it. The possibility that the trip out to Caroline was an exciting assignment compared to their usual work, and that every available person had bagged a place on it, did, however, cross our minds.

Mike Watts and I soon found ourselves in the newsroom, which had been turned into an impromptu dressing room cum make-up area. The two make-up girls spent about fifteen minutes making us look presentable for camera. First to be interviewed was Dave Asher, who was shown in the studio and interviewed briefly about life on board the ship. The film crew then went around filming the cabins, the record library and the galley, including shots of Caroline Martin preparing that night's dinner. Then it was time for my interview.

I was shown reading a news bulletin, then turning to face the camera to be interviewed, although, since there was no news scheduled at the time I was in fact reading a pre-prepared script into a dead microphone. In my news outro, I was careful to include Caroline's frequency ('The next news on Caroline 558 is at four o'clock') so that viewers would know where to find us on the dial. We had been instructed that, for legal reasons, the BBC could not mention our frequency, but this little plug slipped past the editors and was broadcast when the piece was aired, earning me congratulations from Ronan for my ingenuity.

Simon Potter then asked me dozens of questions, the idea being that they got plenty of material for the interview, then edited out what they didn't want later on. Asked about Caroline's legal status, I described it as being akin to a satellite – broadcasting to the UK from outside anyone's territory. We then chatted about the joys and frustrations of life on board. There then followed a break before Mike Watts's interview, during which the crew were to wander around filming out on deck. For this, it would be necessary for us to switch off our transmitters for a while, as using highly sensitive camera equipment directly under a very powerful broadcast aerial would result in poor picture quality. I slipped down into the transmitter room to switch the three services off, leaving Mike Watts happily chatting away to a TV engineer.

Coming down the stairs into the transmitter hold, I was horrified to discover smoke everywhere, with flames clearly visible through some electrical arcing at the point where the diplexer fed into the through-deck insulator. Parts of this system were still made of plastic since the days of the tower collapse, and spots of flaming plastic were dripping down on to some wooden planking on the floor, setting that alight too. I quickly cut the power to the three transmitters, which stopped the arcing, though it did not reduce the existing fire. I raced back up the stairs and ran over to the others to get help, before suddenly remembering that we had a BBC film crew on board. One hint of disaster on board would attract their attention – and transform their image of the station. So much effort had been put into making everything work faultlessly that we mustn't let them see any problems now.

I quickly found a couple of crew, and quietly instructed them to go down to the transmitter room and gather together fire-fighting equipment, but to wait for Mike before using it. Whatever they did, they mustn't attract any attention.

I then approached Mike Watts, who was just about to do his interview and was surrounded by the BBC film crew. Calling him aside, I whispered into his ear that the transmitter room was on fire, and watched as he politely excused himself for a moment, and strolled nonchalantly out of view. As soon as he was out of sight of the crew, he broke into a run. I kept the BBC people occupied and away from the window while Mike and others scurried across the deck with fire extinguishers. One of the visitors asked about the smoke slowly rising to the sky from the middle of our front deck, and I explained that we had a policy of incinerating all our non-biodegradable rubbish, including waste oil. They were quite impressed with this, and congratulated us on our care for the environment.

How we did it I will never know, but the fire was brought under control and extinguished without the film crew ever knowing anything about it. The damage turned out to be mostly superficial, and Mike, working hard, was able to get Caroline back on the air quickly, although he missed his interview with Simon Potter, who was told that we had a slight technical problem which was keeping Mike away. The BBC finally left at the end of a lovely sunny afternoon, circling the ship several times to get shots of it against the sunset. We let out a collective sigh of relief and chatted for the rest of the evening about how close the BBC had been to seeing the Caroline ship as a disaster story.

A few days later, the item was broadcast on *Daytime Live*, and we all gathered round the TV in the messroom to watch it. The team had put together a really positive feature on the ship, showing Caroline in a very good light, and our interviews had been very well edited.

Easter itself was now looming, and it was time to put together a weekend of programming to celebrate Caroline's quarter-century of broadcasting in real style. Five days before the Easter weekend, I gathered everyone together in the messroom and explained the plans that had been drawn up by myself and others to make this a very special occasion. Some parts of the Easter weekend, such as a planned Top 1,000 countdown, and the sightseeing cruise on the *Olau Britannia*, were already well known, but a few innovations by Ronan and PM, and some more on my part, had been kept under wraps. Ronan's requirement was for a special commemoration at midday on Easter Sunday, with a fifteen-minute package to include all the different types of jingles used by Caroline and associate stations over the years, the Caroline theme tune, the John Lennon song 'Imagine' and some special announcements on air at exactly midday. As all this was going out, the party of several hundred Caroline supporters would be travelling towards the *Ross Revenge* on the return leg of their *Olau* trip, and our broadcasts would be relayed live on the ferry where Ronan, Peter Moore and John Burch would be cutting a giant Caroline birthday cake. To make sure that the action was co-ordinated precisely, we had detailed instructions of exactly what to play and say from ten minutes to midday to five minutes past.

After going through the plans from Ronan and PM with the crew, I unveiled my own additions to the weekend, which I had kept quiet until now, despite having secretly tried some of them out. Firstly, the Top 1,000 would actually be a Top 1,001, a change made necessary by the fact that Essex Radio, an ILR station, had copied us, and announced their intention to run a Top 1,000 over Easter, some months after we had begun publicising ours. We would be going one better than them, and also mentioning that our top thousand would not contain almost a thousand adverts as well – an annoying feature of the Essex Radio broadcast we hoped to capitalise on.

Throughout the weekend, we would use an old jingle package from the 1970s, regarded by many supporters as Caroline's finest era. In addition, we would use news jingles from the sixties and would have a music bed (background music) underneath the weather at the bottom of every hour, an instrumental version of a jingle from Radio Mi Amigo, a popular Belgian station that had run with Caroline during the seventies in the same way that Radio 819 ran with us now. The jingles, the 'beds' and the special presentation would combine with the music to give a very atmospheric feel to the occasion.

Then I unveiled my biggest surprise – normal rules would go out of the window and the majority of the weekend would be co-presented by pairs of DJs, who could introduce alternate segues, help each other announce just-played or upcoming records, chat together, or discuss the memories evoked by certain pieces of music. Talk was still expected to be a very small part of the weekend, and the spoken links would generally be no longer than a minute, but the conversation and chat would enhance the style of the station on this special occasion. I would work with Caroline Martin, and other pairs would be made up of compatible individuals, such as Rob Harrison and Paul Shelton. Night-time presentation would be as normal, with one person, as we did not have too many people to spare. As it was important that everything ran smoothly, it would also be useful to have two people on air at any one time, to sort out any problems that might arise. Timing would be very important – we would need to finish playing the thousand records at about 6 PM on Easter Monday, to achieve the largest possible audience, so it was very important that things did not get too far ahead, or behind, schedule.

Control of the record library would also be crucial – counting down a thousand tracks, we could not afford to realise suddenly that

Number 1 was missing. Albums and singles needed for any particular section of the chart were to be pulled by a nominated 'puller' at least four hours before play, and left in piles of fifty in the record library, in order of play, with any records absent because albums were needed in another hour clearly marked, with explanations of where those albums could be found.

As an absolute fallback, so as not to disrupt the order of play for every subsequent record if one simply could not be found, there would be ten special classic tracks, not in the Top 1,001, but pulled and ready for play at any point during the weekend, as substitutes.

I was very keen that the celebrations of Caroline's twenty-fifth birthday would be centred on the music that had been at its heart throughout the years, and in this I was supported by the other presenters. We could have just put together historical documentaries about Caroline and batches of old jingles which, played together, would have pleased a few aardvarks, but this would have turned off the casual listener, whereas a music-centred weekend with some old jingles blended in could be a real audience-puller.

Looking at the compilation of the Top 1,001 itself, we had received thousands of suggestions from listeners – far more than we could possibly hope to process into an accurate running order with the time and manpower available. We decided to assemble the Top 1,001 from scratch, reading in each track from each letter from each person, and putting it on a very long roll of continuous computer paper, which was marked with the places one to one thousand. How high or low the track came in the thousand would depend on many factors – its degree of 'classicness', the place accorded to it in the personal top ten sent in by the listeners, the number of listeners who had suggested it (we spent several hours scanning all the letters quickly to get a feel for the more popular songs), as well as to what extent the track had been a 'Caroline' song over the years.

There was another factor which I was keen to include when putting together the running order. Ronan had for months talked to me about something he called 'pleasure points', a system whereby records which went very well together could be included in the format as a pair, with the station running a format of all-time-great segues. Under the current format, this could not easily be achieved and, under any format, would take months of slog to build up, but the Top 1,001 offered us a golden opportunity to put Ronan's idea into practice on a one-off basis, with pleasure points throughout the countdown for many of our listeners. And what better way could we thank him for twenty-five years of Caroline than by adopting his suggestion on its birthday?

We tried to make sure that in many cases we would put two tracks from individual listeners' suggestions consecutively in the countdown. This was subject to their sounding good together, and to them not having already been placed elsewhere in the chart. This would give each listener his or her own personal 'pleasure point' in the countdown.

It took us most of a day to get the Top 1,001 into shape, and particular care was taken in assembling the selections which would be played from fifty through to one. The Number 1 record was chosen in a discussion between everyone on board, at which a number of songs which had occurred very frequently in listeners' letters were put forward and discussed. One of the songs was 'Imagine' by John Lennon, a favourite of Ronan's. The problem with this was that it was too predictable – 'Imagine' had been number one in a Top 500 compiled for the twentieth birthday in 1984 and would come as no surprise to the listeners. It was therefore put as number two. 'Caroline', by the Fortunes, our theme tune, was also voted for by a large number of listeners, but putting it in at Number 1 would have looked a bit conceited to the casual listener and, in any case, it was played on Caroline all the time. This song, too, was placed elsewhere in the Top 10. Another one suggested by many listeners, and at the top of countless personal Top 10s, was 'The Hurricane' by Bob Dylan. A suggestion by my brother and Rob Harrison that this should be Number 1 was greeted with great enthusiasm by everyone on board. Here was a song by a classic Caroline artist, popular through two decades of the station, a song standing for justice, equality and liberty – all the things that Caroline and its ideals of loving awareness were rooted in.

'The Hurricane', though widely known, was not often played on other stations because of its length, but Caroline had always played it, and indeed it was still in the station's classic-tracks rotation. We took a vote on it, and the result was unanimous.

I stayed up all night on the Thursday, checking and double-checking that everything was ready for the following morning, chatting with Dave and Caroline, who were also up through the night, and occasionally wandering around out on deck, thinking. With the frantic preparations over, and time on my hands, I was able to take the time to go to one of my old haunts, the bow of the ship, sit down just outside the lit-up area of the deck, and stare out across the water. The sea and its beauty relaxed me as always, and I started to think about something that had been in the back of my mind for some weeks now.

Radio Caroline's twenty-fifth birthday would be upon us in a few hours' time, and the planning of several months would be put to the test. Caroline had been founded in 1964 by Ronan O'Rahilly, a twenty-four-year-old Irishman, and now in 1989, the station was being run by me – another twenty-four-year-old Irishman. Caroline had always taken on the youngest people in the radio industry and trained them up to professional standards, and it was this constant injection of new blood that had kept it fresh and innovative over the years. Every few years, the older generation of presenters and management would fade away to careers on land, as Peter Phillips, Kevin Turner and Mark Matthews had done, like many before, leaving new people to take over after them. Now, with the exception of the engineers, who were a different case entirely, and Nigel, who had rejoined after a gap of some years, I was the longest-serving person on Caroline, and the only one who had been on it when it had been broadcasting from the Knock Deep, in the days when Caroline had been accompanied by Laser, a mere half a mile away.

All the people who had been with Caroline when I joined it were now either working on land, or vanished from the radio scene altogether. Soon it would be time for me to move on too – not out of anger or despair, as had seemed might be the case at various times in the past, but by choice – a move on, and back to land, because I would have achieved everything that I could with the station, and it would now be time to hand it over to others, and let them have their time. I would soon be twenty-five, and it would make sense to get back into the mainstream of life while I was still young enough for my career break with Caroline not to matter, as far as the rest of my working life went.

Caroline's twenty-fifth anniversary celebrations and the Top 1,001 would be the pinnacle of my time with the station; anything after that could only be an anti-climax. It would make sense for me to bow out gracefully sometime during the coming months, especially as the station was now in a very strong position – the strongest and most secure it had been since before the big mast fell down in November 1987. I could hand over to someone else, leaving them in a good position, and have no regrets.

I more or less settled it in my mind that I would take a break immediately after the Easter weekend, and then return in late April or May for one final short stint, during which I could show others the ropes, transfer power to whoever Ronan wanted as my successor, and enjoy doing programmes and reading news for the final time. With this clear in my mind, I felt a great peace descend on me, and I wandered back into the ship, ready to do battle with the weekend.

Friday morning finally came, and I was around to read the news during the breakfast show, the last normal programme on Caroline before the celebrations began. By just before 9 AM, I was with Caroline Martin in the 558 studio, the first couple of playlists and record piles at the ready, waiting to begin. At 9, the news was introduced with the old sixties jingle, and I came out of it into the Radio Mi Amigo music bed, over which I explained that this was the official start of celebrations, told the listeners how the countdown would progress over the weekend, and introduced Caroline Martin. Then it was into the first of the 1,001 records, and Caroline and I sat back delighted. The weekend had finally begun.

Caroline and I had a really enjoyable programme that morning, as track after track was a classic and the music, mixed with the old Caroline jingles, made things really atmospheric. We seemed to gel very well together, and were told by others on board that our relaxed and friendly conversations to each other and the listener gave the impression of a cosy little three-way chat. It was certainly enjoyed by us, and judging by letters received later, by the listeners too. We were followed by Rob Harrison and Paul Shelton, who also worked well as a team, with Nik Jackson and Coconut coming after them, and again pairing well. All through the day, everyone on board the ship listened intently to the programmes – apart from the feeling of participating in a very special moment in the station's history, the music was just too good to ignore.

The presents and hampers of goodies sent by supporters and members of the Caroline Movement were broken out, and there was a high-spirited, party-like atmosphere all around the ship. We had more food and drink on board than even the previous Christmas, and everyone was tremendously relaxed and happy. With the programmes rolling, the detailed advanced planning paid off, as pile after pile of records was pulled from the computer-generated lists, played on the station in their chart order, and put back. The substitute records proved their worth too, being needed on two occasions when the only copy of a scheduled piece of music inexplicably vanished without trace.

As Saturday evening drew into Saturday night, excitement on board the *Ross Revenge* grew to fever pitch, as the *Olau Britannia*, with more than three hundred Caroline fans on board, was due to pass us just after midnight. Mike Watts worked another of his little miracles that day, managing to find enough extra light-bulbs and wiring to put rows of extra lights all around the outside of the accommodation section, and on the top of the bridge, so that the *Ross Revenge* would be lit up like a Christmas tree when the ferry passed by. The fluorescent lights he put on short poles on top of the bridge did not even need to be connected to a source of electricity – they drew their power from the intense field of radio energy surrounding the ship, and stayed brightly lit as long as we were on the air.

When the *Olau Britannia* came into sight around midnight, it seemed to be headed almost straight for us, its red and green navigation lights clearly visible. As it drew near, it slowed to a crawl, passing barely fifty yards away, and an incredible sight met our eyes. The whole side and top of the ferry seemed to be an explosion of blue flashbulbs. People were waving torches at us, and the sound of hundreds of people cheering and shouting carried clearly across the water. The *Olau Britannia* shone its spotlight over the *Ross Revenge*, illuminating the ship's entire crew, now all out on the back deck, and as it passed by we could clearly see the individual supporters as they waved, shouted, clapped, photographed and waved banners at us. The cheering was so loud that when the presenter on air in the 558 studio opened his microphone to describe the scene, the noise could clearly be heard by people listening on shore.

Up on the bridge a few minutes later, the ferry captain contacted us by ship-to-shore radio, wished us well, and complimented Mike on our lighting display. Ronan and PM were guests on his bridge and we were allowed to speak to them briefly before the ship passed by into the night. The first leg of the *Olau Britannia* cruise had been a success – now we couldn't wait for when they would all pass us again in broad daylight the following afternoon.

Dawn the following morning, however, brought us a completely unexpected setback – thick fog blanketing the Falls Head, reducing visibility to a hundred yards or so. We prayed that the fog would lift when the sun came up, but it didn't, and as we came closer to the afternoon return passage of the ferry, hopes of a sail-past by our supporters began to dwindle. I was on air on 558 through most of the morning with Caroline , and we made the best of the situation, broadcasting many special messages and dedications to the people who we knew were listening on the ferry as it approached. At midday, we had the special commemoration of Caroline's twenty-fifth birthday – I felt honoured to be the one on air as we marked this occasion with a selection of jingles, soundbites and records, tying in with the cake-cutting by Ronan, which would be taking place on the *Olau Britannia* at the same time. We had our own birthday cake on board the *Ross Revenge*, a radio-shaped one baked specially by a listener, and this was cut and handed round.

For the passage of the ferry in the afternoon, an outside broadcast from the back deck via a radio microphone had been rigged up, with Chris Kennedy as our roving reporter, interviewing people out on deck, and describing what he could see as the ferry went by. Unfortunately, what he could see was not much – the mist was so thick that, even though the *Olau Britannia* came very close, we saw them loom faintly out of the fog for only a minute or so before they were swallowed up again. Those on board the ferry must have had an equally unsatisfactory glimpse of us, but at least they had seen the ship in all its glory the night before.

After that, the rest of Easter Sunday was a bit of an anti-climax, though we would be ramping up the tension again the following day as we headed towards 6 PM, and the conclusion of the countdown. The schedule for Easter Monday was to be different, with Dave Asher partnering Caroline Martin in the morning, because I would be hosting the final section of the chart up to number one, partnered by Mike Watts. Mike had not been part of the regular line-up of late, as we had lots of staff, but, as he was the most senior person on board, and had contributed so much to Caroline's climb back from the disasters of 1987, I felt it was fitting that he would be on air at the climax of our celebratory weekend.

Easter Monday dawned bright, calm and sunny. I was up early, to take a walk around the ship, breathing in the crisp morning sea air before starting my morning news shift.

As it turned out, the 9 AM news bulletin was to be my last contribution to the station that Easter, for barely had I finished reading it than the *Polstar* was spotted heading towards us. It came around our stern and tied up to our port side a little before 9.30.

I decided that I would return to shore with the *Polstar*, and spent a frantic hour or so with Coconut, checking that he had all the information, keys and notes necessary to run the station in my absence. Dave Asher and Caroline Martin were also to head for home, and, at about lunchtime we climbed onto the *Polstar*, and cast off, circling the *Ross Revenge* twice, as was the custom, before heading off across the calm blue sea towards France. It was baking hot and unusually calm for March – a lovely day for a tender trip. On board the *Polstar* were some French supporters, so we had plenty of company for the trip.

Before I knew it, we were in Dunkirk, and approaching the cobbled quayside that had been the embarkation point for me on so many of my adventures. It was now a long time since I had first stood on that quayside, as a square, reserved computer engineer who had just thrown in his job, and who had no idea of what lay ahead.

I looked around at the familiar quayside, and at the tender which had taken me to and from the *Ross Revenge* so many times.

Perhaps I would stand here again one more time. Or perhaps I wouldn't.

13

INTERLUDE

Within a few days of my arrival back on land at the end of March, I found myself with much more reason to stay ashore, when a friendship with Donna, a girl I had met the previous summer, developed into something more. Within a couple of months, all thoughts of returning to sea had gone, though I did make one final trip out to the *Ross Revenge* to collect my belongings, and to chat to Nigel Harris, who had taken over my position of programme controller. I even read the news on 558 one last time before returning to shore and the waiting Donna.

Nothing good lasts forever, and even as I was getting my life together on land, the authorities, determined finally to rid themselves of offshore pirate radio, were preparing a series of blows which would, in little over a year, get Caroline off the air for good.

At just after midday on 19 August 1989, with little warning, the *Ross Revenge* was forcibly boarded by armed Dutch coastguard officials, backed up by a team from the Dutch Broadcasting Ministry, and watched by officials of the British DTI.

Caroline was silenced, and within hours the raiders had seized or destroyed all three transmitters, the entire eight-thousand-strong record collection, and the equipment from every studio on board. The ship was left a gutted shell, its crew still on board, but without any of the equipment needed to run even one radio station. The Dutch officials told those on board that if Dutch broadcasts ever came from the ship again, it would be seized and towed away.

The boarding of Caroline in international waters was against all marine law, but the station was powerless to fight government lawyers, who soon had the ensuing legal case tied up in knots. Through vast donations from supporters, and sterling work by Chicago, Caroline returned to the air on 1 October, with a weak signal on 558 that eventually grew stronger, and a tiny record collection that gradually grew bigger.

I returned to it myself for a brief few days in November, but was ill at ease, having gone out there on impulse without discussing it with Donna beforehand. I came off at the earliest opportunity, and was faced with a lost job, a bruised relationship, and criticism from all quarters.

By the spring of 1990, Caroline was on high power with a good signal on 558 once more, but the main damage caused by the raid had been the removal of the Dutch station. Without income from this or the Dutch-backed World Mission Radio, which had also gone, Caroline was in serious financial difficulties, and it was soon off the air due to lack of fuel. The next blow by the authorities came in June 1990, when they licensed a station in London, Spectrum Radio, on 558. Caroline had now lost its frequency as well as its income.

Caroline solved its fuel crisis, and returned to the air in October 1990 on 819 kHz, very weak, and covering quite a small area. The DTI, knowing that they were close to victory, stepped up their harassment of tender-operators on the British side, and PM was unable to secure a new Continental tender. With fuel rapidly running out again, Caroline plunged on into the winter.

One evening in early November 1990, as I drove home from work, Radio Caroline was on the air – the following morning it wasn't, and it was not to be heard in the days that followed. The fuel had run out, this time for good.

January 1991 saw the implementation of the 1990 Broadcasting Act, which gave the British government the power to board and seize ships in international waters if they were broadcasting a signal that could be heard in the United Kingdom.

Ronan was sure that he could come up with a quasi-legal 'licence' from a Third World state, which would allow Caroline to resume broadcasting unmolested, and usher in a new era of prosperity for the station. It was vital, however, that the ship remain out at sea while negotiations were taking place, because if it ventured into UK waters, it would be seized and held indefinitely by the government.

During the summer of 1991, while I was visiting PM, I ran into Ronan O'Rahilly again. Ronan accosted me in the Black Rose and asked if I would be willing to spend a few weeks 'baby-sitting' the *Ross Revenge*. I would be part of the volunteer crew of three or four who kept the ship lit and anchored out at the Falls Head in the hope that Ronan would one day come up with a licence, and start the station up again. Ronan was immensely persuasive, and I eventually agreed to go out for one six-week spell, provided my new girlfriend, Wendy, could come with me.

Wendy and I left our jobs and joined the *Ross Revenge* in late July 1991, and were part of a caretaker crew which included my old colleague from 558 days, Neil Gates. The ship was in a terrible state, having decayed through lack of money and attention, and during the long hot summer days we painted and cleaned wherever we could. It was very strange to be living on the *Ross Revenge* with no radio at all coming from it, or ever likely to, and the only piece of machinery running was a small emergency generator, which gave just enough power for lights and a TV set.

Summer drew on into autumn and winter, and we stayed on board for twelve weeks, returning for another stint in mid-November. Things were getting desperate by this stage – the prospect of a licence seemed no closer, and there were many who believed that the ship, in its weakened position and with no engineers, could never withstand another winter out at sea. Neil was particularly pessimistic and, as winter approached, I too began to feel that I was on a dying ship, the final flickering embers of the great fire that had once been Radio Caroline.

Governments come and go, laws change, but no one can hold out against the forces of nature forever, and the *Ross Revenge* had now been at sea for more than eight years, a longer continuous period than the old Caroline ship, *Mi Amigo*, had managed before it had sunk in a storm. With no fuel reserves, no engineer, no income, and a crew of only six, the situation was hopeless.

And so it was that I came to be on board the *Ross Revenge* on 19 November 1991, Caroline's last ever day of freedom at the Falls Head, and the day that the last remaining pirate radio ship disappeared from the UK coast forever.

14

DIRE STRAITS

19/20 AND 22 NOVEMBER 1991

Dawn came late to the Falls Head that day, a cloudy grey sky blocking the sunlight from the rusty red radio ship. The sea was still and calm, the vaguest of ripples being stirred up by a whisper-soft north-easterly breeze. The only sound was the pitter-patter of a tiny diesel generator down in the bottom of the ship, working away to provide light and basic power.

It was 1,625 days since the *Ross Revenge* had arrived at the Falls Head, bursting with life and hope on that summer day just before the 1987 election. Now the Caroline ship sat at anchor like a ghost, marking time.

In the engineer's cabin at the top of the ship, behind what had once been the newsroom, Wendy and I stirred, and awoke to face another day. The cabin, which used to be the exclusive preserve of Chicago and Mike Watts, was the only one with a double bed, and so we had been allocated it when we arrived out to the ship some months previously.

I peered out through the porthole at the sea around us, surprised to see it still flat calm. All the weather forecasts pointed to this being the day that we would have a major north-easterly storm, so I had been half-expecting to wake up to find it already blowing rough. Perhaps the forecasts were wrong after all and the weather would hold for long enough for another tender to reach us, with the parts that were badly needed for our fast-deteriorating anchor chain.

I went downstairs to the galley, joining new crew member Stuart Dobson, who was making breakfast for himself. As I was cooking breakfast for myself and Wendy, the other three members of our crew surfaced from their cabins – Christian, another volunteer helper; Ricky Jones, a DJ who had joined Caroline not long after I had left; and Neil Gates, who had stayed with the station through thick and thin. We stood around in the messroom, chatting about what the day might bring.

Looking outside, the sky was rapidly darkening, the wind seemed to be getting stronger by the minute, and the Falls Head was looking a very bleak and lonely place. North-easterly gales were always the most violent and were feared on board – it had been a north-easterly which had brought the ship's three-hundred-foot tower crashing down four years earlier – and we were not looking forward to the prospect of facing one now, especially as the repairs which had been long promised to our anchor chain had been stalled yet again by the office on land.

Neil quickly made his way around the ship to ensure that everything was fastened down, while I went to the bow and looked at the chain where it ran off the front of the ship and down into the water. The chain was twisted around itself several times in the few feet of run before it went below the waves, and was obviously twisted under the water too. The *Ross Revenge* turned twice a day on the tide and, somewhere below the waterline, a swivel in the chain had seized up so that the chain no longer turned with the ship, but just twisted itself tighter and tighter. It was essential that a boat with facilities to lift and repair it reached us soon. We had only a few gallons of diesel on board – enough for the little diesel generator which gave us light, but not enough to run the main engine. In any case, the rudder, which had broken some years previously, was now almost beyond repair, with the steering gear in danger of total collapse. If the anchor chain went, we would be on our own.

I went upstairs afterwards, stopping off on the bridge to survey the scene, and make sure that the Falls Head buoy was still visible. It was, just, though most of the time it was obscured by waves. The storm was still getting up, and soon the waves would hide it from view completely, which was a problem, as it was our only visual landmark. The ship's Decca Navigator had long since ceased to function, along with everything else, and was currently showing us in a position ten miles west of Moscow!

Wendy was still quite happy in the cabin, although on getting up to go to the toilet some minutes earlier, she had been thrown across the room and banged her head. I left her at about 3 PM to watch the *Olau Britannia* cross slowly in front of the *Ross Revenge*; the *Olau* was being battered by waves and making heavy weather of its crossing. By now the swell and spray were so high that it was impossible to see the Falls Head buoy, but the ferry would serve as a landmark for now.

As darkness fell, the storm proceeded to get worse, becoming a matter of concern to all the crew. It was now a north-easterly force 9 and still rising, and we had yet to turn and take its full force sideways. The ship began to turn just as Neil was starting to cook dinner an hour or so later; I knew things must be bad when the usually highly independent Neil asked for my help in the galley. It took two of us just to prepare the food because, with the rolling of the ship, we had to use one hand to hang on for dear life, while working with the other. We were having a very hard time just standing upright, never mind preparing food, and just when we thought that things couldn't get any worse, we faced an unexpected setback – the cooking gas ran out.

A trip outside to change the gas cylinders would normally take just one person and about five minutes, but looking through the porthole we could see massive waves hitting us from the front and side of the ship, sending spray through the air all along the starboard deck. Huge waves of water were now breaking over the side, swirling up to a foot deep around the base of the gas cylinders before draining back out through the grilles on the ship's side. At first we decided to postpone dinner for a while, but hunger and the thought of the nice steaks that were sitting in the oven soon made us change our minds. It took the combined efforts of Neil, myself, Stuart and Christian to change the gas cylinder out on deck, and even then it took us almost twenty minutes to do it. The starboard deck was a swirling maelstrom of water, and the roaring of the wind in our ears made conversation impossible. Two people were needed to hold the cylinders steady while Neil swapped over the regulator, and I held Neil in position and stopped him from being swept away. It was with great relief that we returned indoors when the job was finally done. Neil got the cooking going again, and we sat in the messroom, dripping. This would go down in Caroline history as one of *the* big storms.

Later in the evening, I visited Wendy up in our cabin, and found her feeling lonely and frightened, the room slowly coming to pieces around her. I lay beside her for a while, telling her it couldn't possibly get any worse, but she was not convinced. I promised her that I would come to bed and stay with her after I had been downstairs to check that I wasn't needed for anything else. Even as I stood up to go, the rolling was so acute that the carpet was slipping along the floor under my feet, and it was all I could do to stop myself from falling.

On the bridge, I found Ricky hanging on to the ship's compass, peering through the night at the mountainous seas outside. He was trying to see the Falls Head buoy but was unable to do so. Despite some concentrated searching, I couldn't find it either, although with the waves so high, it would be a miracle if we could.

I anxiously scanned the lights of the coast, where the tip of Thanet was just visible occasionally, and checked it against the reading from the compass. I breathed a sign of relief. We were still in position, as far as I could tell. We made our way downstairs, where I ascertained from Neil that I was not needed, and bade the others goodnight. I made my way back upstairs again.

'When is it going to die down?' Wendy asked me. 'It just seems to be getting worse and worse.' I assured her that things would look better by morning, though she told me that she did not believe a word that I was saying. The moaning of the wind through the ship's towers filled our ears, the rolling of the ship from side to side made us struggle constantly to remain in bed, and every now and then a particularly vicious roll and rudder bang would vibrate the entire cabin, and run right through us.

During the night, I heard the phone ring a couple of times, and was able to listen to Neil's side of the conversation as he talked from the bridge. A mobile phone had been sent out to the ship some months previously, though it only worked for incoming calls. As well as the calls, the ship-to-shore radio on the bridge was turned up fairly loud, and I could hear the coastguard trying to contact an unidentified ship which was sailing down the Dover Straits towards the south coast, and was apparently pursuing an erratic course. The identity of the vessel was unknown, and it was not responding to any signals. Judging by the position that the coastguard gave out, this ship was very close to the East Goodwin lightship, and at least fifteen miles away from us, so there would be little chance of our spotting it. I lay awake in the darkness, struggling to shield Wendy from the worst of the rolls, waiting to notice the small decrease in motion that would mean the ship had turned to face into the wind, or that the storm had reached its peak and was beginning to die down.

During the night, there did seem to be the start of a faint improvement. The rolls seemed to be less acute, and the rudder bangs less pronounced. With any luck, things would continue to ease off as we got towards morning, and the storm would have blown itself out by the end of the following day.

Suddenly, things got dramatically worse, however. We must have turned sideways on to the wind and waves again, for the *Ross Revenge* started rolling rapidly, tilting at crazy angles and threatening to upend our little cabin. And then there was a strange sort of double shudder, another vibration through the hull, as if something was smacking at the infrastructure. I was filled with foreboding as I tried to work out what this strange motion could be.

I had been on the *Ross Revenge* through three winters, and innumerable storms, and I knew its every mood and motion. Never before, in the fiercest of north-easterlies, not even in the 1987 hurricane, had it moved in quite this way. Something was definitely wrong. Even as I debated getting up, I was thinking of the anchor chain, and the worn link where it dropped over the bow. Neil and I would have to make a trip to the forepeak at first light, whatever the weather, to assess the situation.

191

Even as I was thinking, there was another strangeness – two rolls to port, which seemed to stop before they should, almost as if there was something out there preventing the ship from riding the swell properly. Before I had even a couple of seconds to assimilate this data, and come to the obvious conclusion, the world fell apart around me.

Riding the crest of an enormous wave, the *Ross Revenge* rolled heavily to port and slammed hard into something solid underwater, with all the force of hundreds of tons of metal hitting a solid brick wall. The ship literally bounced up in the air, catapulting Wendy and me out of bed, and we went flying through the air, landing on the opposite side of the room as the ship went the other way, hard to starboard, and every single fixture and fitting of Chicago's leapt from the benches, snapping the metal restraints, and rained down on the nearly horizontal wall around us.

As the ship went right down, almost flat on its side, there was a mighty roar of tons of equipment and machinery all over the vessel breaking free and crashing into the walls, and then another as thousands of tons of seawater came over the now-submerged starboard deck and hammered its way into the ship, breaking open portholes, forcing open doors, squeezing through every nook and cranny, every fissure in the normally above-decks accommodation part of the ship.

We hung there, the ship almost on its side, for a few seconds, and then slowly she rose again, turning the wall we had landed on back into a wall and not a floor, and there was another rumble of machinery and furniture crashing back down onto the floors again.

The ship resumed its normal rolling and crashed heavily again onto an unseen object, with a tearing, grinding noise, as the hull slid across something obviously very hard – and huge. Wendy and I were on the other side of the cabin from the bed, we were bruised, battered, and covered in loose objects, and we knew that something very serious was going down. I instantly decided to get us out of our now wrecked and lonely cabin, and into the company of the others, where we would at least have safety in numbers, and be able to find out what was happening.

'Get these on,' I said, throwing Wendy a lifejacket and a warm jumper from the pile of belongings on the floor. 'I'll find the others and see what the hell is going on.'

I reached the bridge at the same time as Neil, Christian and Ricky came pounding up the stairs.

'Shit,' said Neil. 'I think we're in trouble.'

'I've never known it this bad,' I said, trying to get across to the bridge windows so I could see outside.

'Neither have I,' said Neil.

'The main corridor's under a foot of water,' Ricky told me. 'It just burst open the hatchway and came in like a solid wall.'

Neil turned to me from the window, his face white. 'Steve, come and look at this coastline. I think we've drifted. Look, it's all different.'

'I can't find the buoy,' said Christian, who was checking our compass and peering out the other side. 'It's just not there.'

The coastline, which for most of the night had been invisible, was clearer now. Rows of yellow street lights could be seen stretching off into the distance, across the sea from our port side. It looked much closer than usual, and the size, the direction . . . it was all wrong.

'There's something off our bow,' said Ricky. 'Here, come and have a look.'

We crowded around him, looking at a white flashing buoy in the distance. It was flashing sporadically, not like the Falls Head one, which flashed in a regular sequence.

'Perhaps it's the Drillstone,' I suggested, referring to a buoy about five miles from the Falls Head, in towards Ramsgate.

We looked at the buoy, and then at the charts, but couldn't be sure. There was little doubt in our minds that the *Ross* had broken its anchor chain sometime during the night and drifted away, but the question was – where? Without our Decca Navigator, we were helpless. There was nothing for it but to call the coastguard, despite all that that entailed for the crew of a pirate ship. Tension mounting, I took the handset of the ship-to-shore radio set.

'Dover Coastguard, this is *Ross Revenge*, do you read us?'

There was no reply.

Neil adjusted the power setting on the radio, and I tried again.

'Dover Coastguard, this is *Ross Revenge*, do you read us?'

'*Ross Revenge*, this is Dover Coastguard – go ahead,' the reply came back crystal clear.

'Yeah, Dover, this is *Ross Revenge*. We were wondering if you could give us a position check, please. As far as we are aware, we should be about one mile south-east of the Falls Head buoy, but we've had it pretty rough for the last few hours, and we cannot find our bearings – over.'

'*Ross Revenge*. This is Dover Coastguard. Go to channel 80, please, and we will DF (find us by homing in on our ship-to-shore radio signal) you.'

I tuned to the new channel, and keyed up the mike again.

'Dover Coastguard, this is *Ross Revenge*. I'll give you a few seconds more of us for you to track – testing 1-2-3-4-5, testing 1-2-3-4-5, this is *Ross Revenge*, over.'

The reply came back from the coastguard instantly, in a very different, and deadly, serious tone of voice.

'*Ross Revenge*, this is Dover Coastguard – can you tell us please how many people you have on board?'

The words cut through us like a knife. We knew from the tone of the voice, and the question asked, that we must be in serious trouble. The only reason they would ask how many of us there were would be if they needed to know how many people they had to rescue.

'We have six crew aboard,' I replied.

'*Ross Revenge*, do you have any idea . . . have you any knowledge of the situation that you are in?' asked the coastguard.

'Er . . . we had a bit of a bang a few minutes ago, and thought that something might be wrong, and couldn't find our bearings, which is when we called you.'

'*Ross Revenge*, we believe you are aground on the Goodwin Sands. I repeat, you are aground on the Goodwin Sands – a helicopter has been scrambled to you, do you wish to come off?'

'Can you say again,' I asked, not because I had not heard, but because my brain needed more time to take in what he had said to us.

We couldn't be . . . the Goodwin Sands was almost eighteen miles away from the Falls Head – and the most deadly spot for shipwrecks off the entire southern English coast. We couldn't have drifted eighteen miles without realising it. We just couldn't.

'Yes, *Ross Revenge*, we have located you. You are aground on the Goodwin Sands, I repeat, aground on the Goodwin Sands. Do you wish to abandon ship?'

'Hang on, Dover – I'm alerting the crew,' I responded, stalling for time.

No one on the *Ross Revenge* needed to be told about the Goodwin Sands, and its reputation as the 'great ship swallower', where hundreds of ships and thousands of men had ended their lives after running aground in storms. Any other captain, or any other crew, would have abandoned ship immediately. But we were a Caroline crew, and within moments we had all backed Neil's decision to stay aboard, and to try and salvage the ship, and the situation, for the future of Radio Caroline. If we lost the ship, we lost everything . . . Neil took charge, and ordered us all into lifejackets, and while the others were going down to their cabins to fetch theirs, I sounded the continuous tender bell – the alarm signal, which had never had to be used, apart from in drills, until this moment.

Soon, everyone, including Stuart, who had been alerted by the bell while down in his cabin, was back on the bridge, all dressed in lifejackets. Neil and I checked them to make sure they were on correctly, then checked each other's. An RAF helicopter arrived above us, its blades almost inaudible in the storm, and caught the ship in a powerful spotlight. Dover came on the radio again, asking us to abandon ship, and we told them that we were going to stay, and try to get the ship out of danger if we could. The helicopter was stood down, and flew away, Dover promising that the Ramsgate lifeboat would be sent out in its place, to drop anchor nearby and rescue us at the first sign of trouble.

Having made our decision to stay and save the ship, which was rapidly battering itself to pieces underneath us, the next decision was how to do it. We had no way of contacting the organisation on land, and even if we had, there was little hope that they would be able to assist us quickly. We needed a salvage tug to pull us off the sands before the ship capsized or was smashed to pieces, and we needed it now. The ship-to-shore radio sprang to life again with a message from the coastguard.

'*Ross Revenge*, do you want us to send out a tug from Dover to assist you?'

We knew exactly what these words meant. A tug from Dover would mean a tow to Dover if we got the ship free from the Goodwins, and the arrival of the *Ross Revenge* in a British port would mean a massive salvage fee to get it back, probable detention by the British government – victory for the authorities, in other words. But without a tug, the *Ross* would start to settle into the sands, digging a hole for itself within hours, breaking its back and sinking within days . . . if it didn't capsize and kill us all first. Within a few hours, she could be so deeply buried in sand as to be beyond help. (The Goodwin lightship, when it broke anchor and grounded on the sands in the 1950s, had been beyond rescue after only two hours.) A sunken ship would be worth even less to Caroline than a captured one.

We talked about the situation quickly, and I remembered the last drifting in 1988, when it had been almost a week before the organisation had raised the money to send a friendly tug out to help us. And that had been in the good old days.

Accepting a British tug would be a terrible gamble, but perhaps our only hope. We agreed, and told the coastguard that we wanted the tug.

'*Ross Revenge*, the tug will be with you within the hour' came the reply. 'Ramsgate lifeboat will be with you shortly. Keep in contact, Dover out.'

After this exchange, we stood around and took stock. We had hit the sandbank and nearly rolled over at 3.50 AM. It was now 4.15. It would not be dawn for a long time yet and the storm raging outside was still savage. Swell from the north-easterlies was still lifting the *Ross Revenge* up, hammering it down again on the hard sand, driving us further onto the sandbanks, with much tearing and scraping along the hull each time it did so. We organised ourselves into pairs, Ricky and me going down to the depths of the engine room to check the level of water in the bilges. If we were holed, it would be rising – and we would be in trouble.

Down in the very bottom of the ship, we were right above the grounded section of hull, and could hear the scraping and grinding magnified all around us. Each time we slammed down on the bottom, it seemed as if the floor beneath us was about to give way. Way down here, if the ship rolled over, we wouldn't have a hope in hell of getting free.

Luckily, the water in the bilges was at the normal level, and we quickly made our way upstairs to give this news to Neil. The main levels we passed downstairs were a mess – several inches of water still in the main corridor, the galley totally flooded, the messroom carpet sodden from waves which had sprayed through the edges of the still-sealed portholes. Back upstairs, we found Neil talking to the coastguard again, giving them our mobile-phone number so that the salvage tug *Dextrous* from Dover could call us direct. The coastguard agreed to call someone on shore for us, to alert our organisation to the plight of the ship.

We quickly took a call from the Dover Harbour Board, who wanted to know if we were willing to sign the standard Lloyds salvage agreement, and then another call came from Caroline supporter John Knight, who had been roused from his bed by a call from the coastguard. John was involved with a group of enthusiasts called the *Ross Revenge* Support Group, whose aim was to help Caroline keep the ship at sea; he promised to do all he could for us.

Our little generator was still running at full tilt, providing us with light and power, despite the fact that it was situated directly underneath a leaky hatch on the front deck, and water must have been literally cascading down on top of it. I went into the newsroom, where an electrical control panel was situated, and switched on as many exterior spotlights as I dared, so that our rescuers or helpers would have light to work with. The generator struggled with the extra unexpected load, and the lights dimmed for a moment, before coming back up again. Visibility started to improve, and we were now able to see the East

Goodwin lightship, about two miles away, and, further off in the same direction, the lights of France. Huge waves were still coming towards us from the north-east, lifting us up, then breaking into smaller waves near our stern, which seemed to be the part of the ship that was aground. The bow rose and fell, twisting from side to side, but the stern was now firmly embedded in the underwater sandbank – putting who knows what stresses and strains on our hull.

At 6 AM, we heard a news report about our grounding on Invicta Radio, but there was still no sign of the promised tug. Dover Coast-guard told us that it was on its way but was not now due for another hour.

As the time went by, and there was no sign of the tug, we began to feel more and more isolated and vulnerable. The *Ross*, after a period of relative stability, started twisting and banging on the bottom again, with such ear-piercing metallic scrapes and thuds that we felt it must surely spring a plate at any moment. Neil, Ricky and I went downstairs again, checked the bilges, and examined the main level. As the ship rolled and thumped around in the water, and the waves hit us, the amount of water making its way in had begun to increase, and the cor-ridors and floors were under an inch or so of water again. In particu-lar, water was forcing its way up through drains, perhaps propelled up as we smacked against the bottom, and this was causing considerable flooding. Only the messroom seemed safe and relatively dry.

A quick ring on the tender bell summoned us, and we returned upstairs, leaving behind the relative calm of the messroom again. The bell had been rung by Christian and Wendy, who had had a message from the coastguard, telling us that the tug was delayed again and would not arrive until well after 7 AM. Our morale sank through the floor.

Suddenly, the ship was lifted up in a massive wave and came crash-ing down onto the sandbank, with a bumping, grinding noise, and made an alarming lurch to one side. The ship settled again, down at least fifteen degrees to starboard, and did not right itself. Another wave took us, there was another series of bangs and bumps, enough to throw us off our feet, and when we got up, we were further down to starboard than before. Wave after wave came towards us, and each one left us a little closer to being on one side. The horrifying thing was that the ship was not even trying to right itself again.

'That's it,' said Neil. 'We're coming off.'

No one disagreed.

Neil rushed to the radio set. 'Ramsgate lifeboat, this is *Ross Revenge*, we now wish to abandon ship.'

'*Ross Revenge*, this is Ramsgate lifeboat, we will be with you shortly.'

'*Ross Revenge*, this is Dover Coastguard, helicopter has been scrambled.'

Another wave, another lifting of the ship, and we banged ferociously on the bottom again, ending up further over on one side. It was now quite difficult to stand upright on the steeply sloping floor, and the churning sea visible through the starboard bridge windows was getting closer and closer.

Suddenly, there was a noise like thunder from the top of the bridge, and the windows of the two doors leading out onto the back deck turned white, in the most concentrated hail of spray I had ever seen. We all looked at each other, our fear mounting. Whichever way we got off the ship, we would have to go outside – which meant braving that spray, which was now coming in concentrated bursts, every time the stern slammed down into the shallow water, like a boot smashing down into a puddle.

Wendy clutched me tightly. 'We won't have to go out there, will we?' she asked

'We might have to,' I replied.

'I don't much fancy it myself,' said Neil. 'But . . .' and then another wave tilted us further over, another resounding bang on the bottom took us off our feet, and a monsoon of spray swept across the ship and hammered on the roof. We struggled to our feet again, clinging to whatever we could to keep our balance.

'Come on, come on, where is that lifeboat?' cursed Neil.

'*Ross Revenge*, this is Ramsgate lifeboat, have you a lee side?'

We peered out into the first light of dawn, and could only see massive breakers and churning water all around us. We told the lifeboat to come on our starboard side, as it was so far down now that we'd have less distance to jump from there. They agreed, and added that they were just moments away.

We were taking an incredible pounding now, juddering up and down on the bottom, the sound of tortured metal from underneath us competing with the blasts of spray thundering over the metal decks. Jumping onto a lifeboat in these conditions would be almost suicidal, but what choice did we have?

The lifeboat rounded our stern, and attempted to come towards us. It was still a hundred yards away when it was caught up by a big wave, and hurled sideways in the water.

'It's gone over,' shouted Christian. 'The lifeboat is on its side.'

I climbed back up the floor to the ship-to-shore radio, bracing myself against an instrument console.

'Ramsgate lifeboat, this is *Ross Revenge* – are you all right?'

There was nothing but silence.

'Ramsgate lifeboat, this is *Ross Revenge*, are you all right?'

There was silence for a long moment, then a reply. 'Yes, *Ross Revenge* . . . This is Ramsgate lifeboat . . . Hang on, I'm checking with my coxswain . . . Yes, *Ross Revenge*, this is Ramsgate lifeboat – we have run aground.'

Fear clutched tight at our throats, as we took another huge wave, and were battered down again, the ship now tilting at a thirty-five-degree angle. We were stuck fast on the Goodwin Sands, the tug no where in sight, smashing ourselves to pieces, probably moments away from rolling over. Now our rescuers were stuck too. Neil grabbed the radio from me and asked how long it would be until the helicopter reached us.

'Ten minutes' came the reply, as we went over even further.

We all looked around and at each other, suddenly realising that we would be lucky to get out of this alive. The ship was going over too fast, and soon we would be on our side, and hurled out into the icy water. The irony was that although there was not enough depth for the *Ross*'s considerable draft, there was more than enough to fill her up if we went sideways – and more than enough to drown in.

'Everybody get over to the port side,' Ricky called. 'If we go over, it may still be above water.' Another huge wave was heading towards us.

Neil looked at me with a sudden intensity. We had been through so much together, had worked together for so long over the years. I knew what he was about to say, and a chill went through me even as he started to say it.

'Steve . . . I just want to say . . . Steve, well . . . It's been great . . . Goodbye, Steve.'

'I hope we can make it, but if we don't, it's been . . . a pleasure to know you. Goodbye, Neil, and everyone, it's been . . .'

'No!' Wendy almost screamed, clinging to me so tightly her nails were piercing the arm of my shirt. 'Tell me it's going to be OK.'

I wanted to tell her, but I couldn't lie. All I could do was hold her tightly and tell her I loved her, and then the wave was on us.

'Stand by, this may be it,' I told them.

As we were lifted yet again, a million thoughts went through my mind. I thought how, in twenty-seven years, no one had ever been killed or injured on a Caroline ship – and now it was all going to end with the six of us drowning in icy water. I lost my footing and was flung across the bridge, landing in a corner near the rapidly tilting starboard windows. The electrics of the ship-to-shore radio set sparked alarmingly, as spray forced itself onto the bridge. We were over by more than forty degrees now. I managed to make it to the radio set, and told the coastguard that communications might become impossible at any moment, as our ship-to-shore set was in danger of failing. They asked us to launch a life-raft. We looked out onto the back deck, but could see no way of getting a life-raft into the water, and then jumping in after it, without being swept away.

'We'd be washed away,' I told them.

'Helicopter will be with you soon – tug *Dextrous* and any other vessels in the area – you may have to search for bodies in the water.'

The six of us – the bodies he was referring to – looked at each other in horror. Dawn was breaking fully now, and we could all see the churning, bubbling mass of sea around us, where strange currents created by the shifting sands, and the massive breakers, combined to make the water look mad with rage. We wouldn't last a minute in that.

'God bless you and protect you, *Ross Revenge*, you were the good guys,' said an unknown voice on the radio, the crew of a ship somewhere out there listening in to our drama and wishing us well.

Another huge wave was coming.

'*Ross Revenge*, this is Rescue Helicopter 166, we will be with you in two minutes,' came the reassuring voice of an RAF pilot. Even as he spoke, we could hear the helicopter's massive rotor blades as it passed overhead, and could see it settle into position a hundred feet above our stern. Maybe we were going to get out of this alive after all.

'Right, we are abandoning ship now – out this way,' Neil called, opening the bridge door out onto the little balcony leading to the back deck. We formed a human chain and struggled out into the wilderness.

Once outside, the wind and chopper noise deafened us, and within seconds we were soaked to the skin, and almost blinded by spray. We edged our way down the stairs onto the back deck, looking with horror at the seething seawater just a few feet away below us, waves breaking over what had been the starboard deck, and pounding the side of the ship. The back deck was tilting and jumping beneath us, as if wanting to throw us into the sea, and we reached the base of the back tower, and grabbed it, huddling around it for support. The stern kept smashing down into the water, sending spray so dense hurling over us that we could not even see each other. The wind and spray made it difficult to breathe, and within moments we had swallowed so much spray that we felt sick. We were frozen stiff, drenched and disorientated, but we managed somehow to cling to the tower, without which we would surely have been washed overboard.

The helicopter approached, lowering a winch man. Neil and Wendy went to him first. When he came down again, the winch man signalled for Ricky and me to go next, and we set about trying to cross the few yards of back deck separating us from the stern, where the winch man was. We dashed halfway, pausing to grab a stay, just before the ship reeled again under us, and a massive wave broke over us, leaving us blinded, retching and frozen once more. Another dash brought us to the stern, where the winch man swore at us for taking so long, while quickly strapping a safety harness over our lifejackets.

We felt the beginnings of another earthquake-like smack onto the seabed beneath us, and then we were in the air, just as the spray attacked us again. My body like ice, and my lungs filled with seawater, I had a brief glimpse of the back tower and some stays slicing through the air right in front of me.

I banged my head against something solid in the air above me, and the next thing I knew, strong hands were pulling me into the helicopter and ripping the harness from me, to send it below again for the others. I was grabbed by a burly airman and strapped into a seat on one side of the chopper, beside Neil and Wendy. Ricky was soon plonked beside me. As soon as Christian, Stuart and the winch man were on the end of the rope, the helicopter turned and left the scene, starting the flight back to Kent even as the three were being hauled up through the air. As we turned towards the shore, I had one last glimpse of the *Ross Revenge* at sea, trapped in the middle of a boiling mass of water, huge waves breaking over her, tilting at a fifty-degree angle, and lit up by lights and spotlights.

As we flew away from her, she was still semi-upright in the water, somehow managing to look sad, abandoned, and beautiful all at the same time.

* * *

It took more than forty-eight hours, two huge salvage tugs, and four Harbour Board crews to pull the battered radio ship, which refused to sink, off the Goodwin Sands.

Two and a half days later, rested but not recovered, Neil Gates, Wendy and I were driven by police and Customs officials to the ferry port of Dover, where the last of the tugs had just succeeded in tying up the *Ross Revenge*. It was ironic that she had come in onto one of the ferry berths – as we were driven in silence through the eastern docks, I remembered my first ever trip out to Radio Caroline, in a car with the manic Cosmic, passing through this very spot, hoping that Customs would not suspect that we were on our way to the *Ross Revenge* and

Radio Caroline. Here we were again, only this time we were hemmed in by the police, Customs were waiting for us, and everybody knew exactly what we had been up to – and, worse still, with the ship in chains, they now had the power to stop us.

As we pulled up on the quayside, it was heartrending to see the *Ross Revenge*, looking so small and cold and frail, tied up by the quayside that was normally used for giant superferries. There were police and customs officers all over her, on every deck, in every window, poking and prodding, searching and ripping away at the fabric of Caroline.

We knew, without saying it, what was ahead of us – the official detention order on the ship, the massive salvage bill, the endless inspections aimed at preventing her from ever escaping from British jurisdiction. We paused for a moment, halfway up the gangplank. Behind us, down on the quayside, we could see that Chicago and Peter Phillips had arrived, and were being turned away by two policemen, who were telling them that they had no right to come any closer. In front of us were the Customs officers and police, and Department of Transport officials, waiting to question and possibly arrest us, and place the ship under official detention.

After all the years of freedom in international waters, the countless thousands of hours of voices spoken and songs spun across the ether by the ship and her crew, the day of reckoning had arrived. I looked at the others and smiled weakly.

'It's time to face the music,' I said.

Epilogue: The New Radicals

October 1998–August 1999

Improbably, some would say impossibly, both the ship and the station survived to lead a different kind of life.

The ship was officially detained by the British government, and remains so, but negotiations with the authorities eventually led to a truce of sorts, with the authorities allowing the ship to be occupied and used by the radio station and its supporters, provided it does not leave a zone of detention comprising the River Thames and nearby coastal ports.

The station went through the bleakest of decades in the 1990s, during which its flame flickered and was nearly extinguished. It was kept alive only by occasional low-powered temporary broadcasts licensed under the RSL (Restricted Service Licence) system. Money was tight, costs were high, and it was only by sacrificing almost everything else in his life that Peter Moore kept the organisation together. I was gone from the scene at this stage, having left in 1992 after a period of living on the ship in Dover docks.

Moore was always looking for ways other than the expensive and often frustrating RSL system to get Caroline back on the air, and he had occasionally been able to rent airtime from various satellite stations, which almost invariably would start letting blocks of airtime as a last resort before they went bust.

In the autumn of 1998, Caroline was offered some regular weekend airtime by the satellite station EKR, and there seemed no reason to believe that this venture would be any longer-lasting than the others. EKR were themselves struggling for survival, and were offering the airtime at a ridiculously cheap rate, so the station was back on the air again, broadcasting from EKR's base at Maidstone TV studios, every Sunday from 9 AM to 6 PM. Out of the blue, I found myself asked to do programmes. It had been a long time, but I was back on Caroline again.

The other presenters on Caroline's Sunday satellite service were people who had worked on the *Ross Revenge* in the 1980s, including Johnny Lewis and Nigel Harris. Nigel I knew well, having spent a number of stints out at sea with him, but Johnny was from before my era, though we knew each other as members of the extended Caroline 'family'.

Another DJ who joined the satellite service at the same time as myself was someone who I had encountered in my earliest days on the *Ross Revenge*: Dave Foster. Dave had been an overnight and evening DJ on Caroline 558 during my second stint onboard in early 1987, and although our shifts meant that we hadn't got to know each other well, we nonetheless found ourselves with a lot of shared memories to discuss about the days in the Knock Deep.

Having got used in 1991 and 1992 to the ship without the station, I now had to get used to the station off the ship – which was strange.

Technically, it would have been possible to link from the ship, now anchored just off Queenborough on the Isle of Sheppey, to Maidstone Studios, but it would have been enormously expensive, and we just did not have the money to do it.

The new year of 1999 dawned with a development that seemed certain to put Caroline off the air and return it to its mid-1990s status as an occasional RSL broadcaster. EKR, like so many satellite stations before it, was going under, and would close after the end of transmissions on 3 January. It was a very sombre Caroline team that turned up at Maidstone Studios that Sunday morning. EKR had only announced the news the night before, so there had been no time to plan for the closure or to get used to the idea that this would be our final day, and our last chance to speak to the audience we had built up across Europe.

Johnny Lewis was in fighting spirit, and told the audience that somehow Caroline would get back on air on satellite, maybe even from these very studios, on this channel, the following week. Johnny's mood was infectious, and although I had been thinking that there was nothing we could do about the closure, Johnny convinced me, and the others, that we should not take it lying down.

Johnny's suggestion was that Caroline should approach Flextech, owners of the studios and satellite uplink, and ask to rent the studios and airtime that EKR had been using. We would pay monthly in advance, and hopefully, as we were a better-known station than EKR, we would be able to attract more advertising, and make the service pay its way.

Dave and Nigel brought Caroline to a close at 6 PM, while EKR presenter Mark Stafford closed that station a little later. Early the following day, Johnny Lewis made contact with Flextech and arranged a meeting, which Peter Moore also attended.

Flextech were at first sceptical about getting involved with another satellite radio station. However, Peter, backed up by Johnny Lewis, who could point to his own successful radio career, which had been launched by Caroline, persuaded Flextech at least to think about allowing Caroline to use the airtime. The conditions would be tough, though: Caroline would have to pay three months in advance, and would have no security of tenure on the channel.

Over the next few weeks, Dave worked to get equipment together, while I sold some advertising and Peter Moore worked tirelessly to raise the additional funds that were needed, as well as finishing contractual negotiations with Flextech and the Radio Authority (RA). The RA was involved due to the fact that we would be the main broadcaster on the satellite channel rather than just a sub-lessor: we would now have to have our own broadcasting licence.

Delivering the application to the RA head office in Holborn late one afternoon, I mused on just how far we had come from the days when all we needed to do to get Caroline on the air was to trot down the stairs to the transmitter room and flick the switch on the 558 transmitter.

On 20 February, our new studio was buzzing with people, and at 11 AM Caroline burst back onto the air after a six-week absence, to the sounds of popping champagne corks and much cheering. At 5 PM I started my own programme. It was great to be back on the air again, and I sailed through the four hours as if on wings. The playlist was great, combining the great tracks that Caroline used to play in the off-shore days with breaking new material.

Much more so than when broadcasting via EKR, it felt right. This time, Caroline was master of its own destiny, and best of all, we would be back the following day to do it all over again.

The next day, I got a phone call from a familiar voice: 'Stevie baby, hey - so the wanderer returns. It's nice to hear you back on Caroline.'

It was great to talk to Ronan O'Rahilly again: it had been seven years since our last meeting, and I had missed his charismatic personality and his gift of inspiring even the most downhearted. Ronan congratulated me on my return to the station, and on helping get Caroline back on the air. (I'd secured advertising from Grundig.)

The response from listeners to the relaunch of Caroline on satellite was good, and the Caroline Support Group gained a number of new subscribers, as well as considerable additional sales of merchandise. This went some way towards satisfying the people who had worried about the money that had been spent to get the service on the air.

Over the weeks and months that followed, Caroline broadcast every weekend on the Astra satellite. Despite our worries, we managed to make enough money from advertising not only to keep going but gradually to extend our broadcasting hours.

I had already planned that later in 1999 or early in 2000 I would be moving back to Ireland, but I wanted to hang around until at least September, as Caroline was planning a twenty-eight-day medium-wave RSL broadcast from the ship for later in the summer. I was really enjoying the satellite programmes, and broadcasting once again from the ship on a daily basis would be an excellent way to end my years with Caroline.

The RSL broadcast would be from Southend, with the ship moored right at the end of the famous mile-long pier, giving easy access to the station for listeners – and the possibility of big sales of merchandise to the thousands of people who visited the pier every day in high summer. Dave Foster and I were going to be living on board the ship for the entire month of the RSL, along with new DJ Sarah Miles and a few others.

Arriving back on board was like coming home. The ship was alive and humming with power, people were rushing everywhere, the studios were in use and music could be heard everywhere. How much better an arrival on board this was for me than the dark days of 1991.

The twenty-eight days passed in a blur. Every morning I was up before 5 AM to present the breakfast show, being followed on air by Dave Foster. The afternoons were spent showing the considerable crowds of visitors around the ship, and the evenings in scripting and making commercials, which were coming in increasing numbers.

Dave Foster, Sarah Miles and myself co-hosted the final programme on the RSL, and finally closed down at six minutes past midnight – an unintentional overrun due to a wonky clock, which made us into accidental pirates again for the last couple of songs!

We trooped down the stairs and along the corridor to the mess room, to unwind after the frenetic final twenty-four hours. As we walked in, the phone was ringing. It was Ronan. 'Hey, Stevie baby, that was amazing. You handled it brilliantly. You just poured out the good vibes and the loving awareness, man.'

'I didn't know you were in the area,' I told him. (He must have been, to be able to pick up the broadcast.) 'Why don't you come and see us?'

'Well, no, I can't actually do that,' Ronan replied. 'I'm in a club in Kensington at the moment.'

'But how did you hear us then?'

'Hey, don't get hung up on the whole hearing-things-with-your-ears thing. That's what they'd like to tell you: that you can only hear things with your ears. This is Caroline, baby, and you hear it with your soul, Steve, you hear it with your soul.'

WHERE ARE THEY NOW?

RADIO CAROLINE is still on the air today, and in February 2009 celebrated the tenth anniversary of its rebirth on satellite. The station broadcasts on channel 0199 on the Sky system, and can also be heard via the internet.

THE *ROSS REVENGE* has survived and is being preserved by the Radio Caroline Society in remembrance of its days as an offshore pirate ship. It is still used on special occasions as a base for the satellite broadcasts. *www.radiocaroline.co.uk* is the website for the station and the ship, and carries a full range of Caroline merchandise commemorating all eras of the station, as well as a listen-online facility.

STEVE CONWAY now works in Dublin for the rock station Phantom 105.2FM, itself a former pirate, and blogs at *http://steveconway.wordpress.com*. Steve has also put together a website to complement this book, with extra photos and and updates on some of the other people featured, along with off-air clips illustrating some of the incidents described, at *www.shiprockedbook.com*.